Praise for
Unlimited
Referrals

"The success I am having with your referral system is phenomenal. Within one month of your seminar for our company, I converted seven referrals into clients. As I provided great value and service, those seven new clients put over $21,000 in my pocket. And that doesn't even account for the new referrals they are now giving me. Thanks!"

Andrew Monsour, Financial Advisor
American Express

"Every now and then a book arrives on the scene that is destined to change the way we look at selling. *Unlimited Referrals* by Bill Cates is such a book. Give a copy to everyone of your salespeople and watch your company grow."

Ron Lanio
President, Cadmus Promotional

"The top 10% of all salespeople make 50-100% of their sales through repeat business and referrals. Bill Cates shows you all the secrets of getting and converting referrals into more sales. With Bill's powerful system, there are no more cold calls, only warm leads. It's a 'must read' for anyone in business."

Dr. Tony Alessandra
Author of *Non-Manipulative Selling* and *The Platinum Rule*

"*Unlimited Referrals* is full of ideas and strategies that will work for you. It's a winner. Buy it!"

Joe Girard,
"World's Greatest Salesman"
Guinness Book of World Records

"I've already started applying a few of your many ideas. I have encountered very little resistance with your approach. When I call my new prospects, they are <u>expecting</u> my call! Thank you, thank you, thank you."

William King
Northwestern Mutual Life

"Bill Cates has given us a vision for how to be the best, most successful sales professionals possible.

"Not a gimmick, not a technique, but rather the result of a time honored process, the referral is the reward of every successful professional experience. In *Unlimited Referrals,* Bill clearly tells why you should expect more referrals and demonstrates how you can get them. Our salespeople have more confidence and a vastly improved commitment to sell with 'purpose.' If you want more sales with less effort, if you want to learn the skills, and if you want to develop the attitudes that insure you will get the referrals you deserve, this book is exactly what you need."

George Considine, Sales Manager
Harbor Duvall Graphics

"Your system for generating referrals really works. I thought I was doing pretty well before I learned your strategies. Now I can't believe how effective I've become at generating a constant flow of high quality referrals. My listings have gone up and my sales have increased.

"I think everyone in my industry should read your powerful book."

Kay Baer, Real Estate Agent
RE/MAX 100

Unlimited
Referrals

Secrets That Turn Business Relationships Into Gold

by Bill Cates

Referral Coach International
(Thunder Hill Press)
Silver Spring, Maryland

CREDITS:
Editing: Judith Gallagher
Cover Design: Michelle Bailey, ArtLandish! Graphics & Multimedia
Cover Photo: John DeFabbio
Book Design: Bevi Chagnon, ArtLandish! Graphics & Multimedia
Electronic Publishing and Production: Gretchen Muller, ArtLandish! Graphics & Multimedia
Printing: McNaugton & Gunn

ISBN 1-888970-07-3

Referral Coach International
(Thunder Hill Press)
2915 Fenimore Road
Silver Spring, Maryland 20902

Printed in the United States of America
4 5 6 7 8 9 10

Dedication

For my father, Joseph R. Cates, without whose unwavering support, this book would not have been possible. He's my biggest fan. Thanks, Dad!

Acknowledgments

It's impossible to acknowledge all the people who have given me help and inspiration in this project. Here are a few that stand out in my mind: Jenna Catherine Cates, Nancy Bierer, Fred Berns, Gloria Gault Geary, Lynne Waymon, Jeff Salz, Arnold Sanow, David Rich, Terrie Upshur Lupberger, David Lupberger, Sandy Crowe, John Hurley, Randy Richie, Jay Magenheim, Al Lowery, Steve Zerlin, Gary Glaser, Joel Rosenberg, Tony Alessandra, Jim Cathcart, Bob Burg, Patricia Fripp, Wolf Rinke, Scott Kramnick, Bob Sommers, Jerry Hartman, George Considine, Ron Lanio, Phil Boland, Helene Hahn, Dave Kelly, Andrea Scott, and Michelle Lemmons.

Contents

Preface

The Most Important Sales Lesson I Ever Learned

Can you remember the first thing you ever sold? Go way back, into your youth. Was it lemonade? Candy? Cookies? I remember my first experience in selling as if it were yesterday.

I was 9 years old, a Cub Scout (pack 456, den 2, in Kensington, Maryland). Our pack needed to raise money. So we decided to hold a sales contest. The product: furnace filters. The prize: a brand new, shiny, royal blue, 26-inch, three-speed Schwinn bicycle.

Man, did I want that bike. I'd be the first on my block to own a three-speed.

And blue was without a doubt my favorite color. I was currently riding an old, beat-up, rusty-red, 20-inch no-name. Some of my friends even made fun of my bike. Boy, would I be the envy!

I knew I was going to win that bike. I owned that bike in my mind before the first shipment of furnace filters even arrived. I went downstairs to the laundry room and stole a few clothespins from my mother. Then I slipped out a few playing cards from my father's dresser. When that bike arrived, I was ready to add those flipper cards to the rear wheels. That would be my motor. Not only would Billy Cates have the newest, bestest bike in the whole neighborhood, but also I would make sure the whole neighborhood knew it. Varoom!

On July 25th, 1960—the hottest day of the year—the furnace filters arrived. Who in their right mind would try to sell furnace filters in the dead of summer?

Selling door to door appears to be a dying art, and I hope it dies a permanent death. It certainly was a challenge, but it didn't stop me. Even at the age of 9, I knew that selling was only a matter of numbers. If I knocked on more doors than any other scout, I would sell more filters. And that bike would be mine.

Doors were slammed in my face. People who I could see were at home ignored me. The fiberglass filters itched my sweaty skin. But I wanted that Schwinn.

I went up one side of the street and down another. Finally I stood in front of the house at the end of my block that bordered a dead end. The Wilkses lived there: Dimmie and Bill Wilks, with their daughters Adrienne and Sharon. Dimmie and Bill were good friends of my parents. My sister played with Sharon. I was facing their door with dread.

Almost every day during the summer, and many days after school, neighborhood kids gathered in the dead end to play baseball. Third base was on the Wilkses' property. Mr. Wilks didn't like this. We'd be playing in the dead end and he would come around the corner in his yellow Ford Galaxy. He'd flash his lights, honk his horn, and jump out of the car. This signaled the end of the game, because everyone ran. It was so predictable that when we started the game we didn't bother to decide how many innings we'd play. We just played until Mr. Wilks came home from work. Whichever team was ahead when he came home would win.

To me at age 9, Mr. Wilks was the ogre of the neighborhood. And there I stood ready to knock on his door. I was hoping and praying that Dimmie Wilks would answer. When Mr. Wilks opened on the door, I was shaking in my shoes.

He said, "Hi, Billy Cates, what ya got there?"

I gave him my best sales pitch. "I'm selling furnace filters to raise money for my Cub Scout pack. You don't want any, do you?" (Great closing, huh?) "Selling door to door, eh?" he responded. "When I got started in sales, I sold pots and pans door to door. Come on in. I'll take two of those filters if you have the right size."

I couldn't believe it. Not only was I sitting in his living room, but also he was being nice to me, and buying two filters! You see, it turned out that mean old Mr. Wilks was a salesman. He had a very successful career with Hallmark Cards. And he wasn't so mean after all.

Then he said to me, "So, Billy, what's your closing ratio?"

"Huh?"

"How many houses have you visited and how many sales have you made?"

"Oh, well, let's see. I've been to . . . let's see . . . about 10 houses and I've sold filters to two of them."

"Well, that's not bad. Would you like to increase that ratio?"

"I guess so."

"Well, Billy, you need to be selling from referrals."

I looked at him blankly.

"It's simple, son. The house across the dead end is owned by Mr. and Mrs. D'Angelo. When they answer the door, you say that Mr. Wilks recommended that you talk to them about your furnace filters, and that I bought two. With me so far?"

"Yes."

"Then as you are leaving, ask them the names of their neighbors and ask if they think you should call on them. Repeat this with every house. Think you can do that?"

"I'll try."

So off I went. I was driven to win that bike, and now I had a technique to help me. Mrs. D'Angelo answered the door. I said, "Hi, I'm Billy Cates from up the street. Mr. Wilks said I should talk to you. I'm selling furnace filters to raise money for our Cub Scout pack. Mr. Wilks bought two. How many would you like?" (I was working on my closing too.)

Mrs. D'Angelo bought one filter and gave me the name of her neighbor. I was off and running. Do I have to tell you who won that contest?

I was so focused, so driven, and so well trained that I sold more filters than the entire pack of 38 boys combined. I won a new set of wheels!

I still own that bike. I keep it at my dad's house, in the basement. Whenever I think the odds are stacked against me, whenever I think I won't be able to reach a goal, I pay a visit to my father. I drag out that not so shiny, royal blue, 26-inch, three-speed Schwinn bicycle. I ride it up and down the block a few times, making sure to ride by Mr. Wilks's house to give him a grateful salute.

I won that sales contest because I was able to harness two critical elements to success in sales: a burning desire and an effective strategy. I can't give you the burning desire. You either have it or you don't. But this book is filled with strategies that can fire it up again.

That first experience in sales taught me that the most powerful way to sell just about anything is through referrals (and related strategies). My success has been based on a referral mindset. I create relationships of trust and friendship. Then I leverage those relationships to create winning situations for all parties. I give others help, and I ask for their help.

There are two things that all successful people have in common. First, they have long necks. That's right. All successful people have long necks. They're willing to "stick their necks out" and take the risks necessary to get better all the time. Second, they know that anything worth accomplishing can't be done alone. They form good working relationships with others, and they leverage those relationships for the benefit of all.

That's what this book is all about: forming great relationships, leveraging those relationships for mutual benefit, and constantly taking small risks to improve yourself.

Introduction

You've Just Struck Gold!

I was going to title this introduction "Why I Wrote This Book." Then my sales and marketing brain kicked in and said, "Talk about benefits to the readers." So in a minute I'm going to tell you why you made a great decision in picking up this book. First, I'd like to tell you briefly why I wrote it.

It's simple, really. I've been using the principles, strategies, and skills in this book for years, and they've helped me build my success. I've been sharing them through my presentations to salespeople, sales managers, and business owners for several years. Now I'm truly excited about how I've put all the information together. This book is the blueprint you need to build as big a business as you desire. You've just struck gold!

Why is referral selling the most powerful way to sell?

Without question, selling through referrals is the most powerful way to build your business, not to mention the most enjoyable. There are a few rare birds out there who really love prospecting for business through cold calls. My guess is that if you're reading this book, you're not one of them. In this age of voice mail, increased competition, and super-busy prospects, cold calling has become less effective.

I once heard Robert Kerrigan (a legendary salesperson with Northwestern Mutual Life) say, "The way of the world is meeting people through other people." And the referral is the warm way we get into their lives.

Think about this for a minute. When you need to find an attorney, an accountant, a car repair shop, or a dentist, do you turn to the Yellow Pages? Probably only as a last resort. Don't you usually ask a few friends first? Why? Because you'd rather not "buy cold." You'd rather be referred.

Buyers too prefer not to buy cold. There's more tension. There's more risk. I'm not saying that cold calls never work. However, it's getting harder to reach people with them, and cold calling can lead to early burnout if it's your only prospecting strategy.

 Chris Faicco, with Northwestern Mutual Life, conducted the only study I know of that clearly demonstrates the power of referrals. Of 5,640 qualified suspects, 2,240 were turned into prospects by cold calls, and the remaining 3,400 were converted into prospects by referrals. The cold call prospects yielded 56 sales, or an 11 percent closing ratio. The referral prospects yielded 452 sales, or a closing ratio of 40 percent. In this study, the chances of making the sale were almost four times greater when the prospecting was done from referrals.

If you don't sell life insurance, you may be thinking, "What does this have to do with me?" Everything. Oh, the ratios in your industry may be a little different. But you wouldn't be reading this book if you didn't already have a clear sense that building your business from referrals is the best way.

Why do referrals lead to sales faster and more easily?

When you prospect over the telephone via cold calls, you usually get the cold shoulder. The prospects say things like, "Send information." "I'm already covered in that area." "We're happy with our current supplier."

When you prospect over the telephone via referrals, you usually get a conversation. Two elements make this so. First is commonality. The fact that you and your prospect know someone in common warms up the conversation from the very beginning. Usually, the better the relationship between your referral source and your new referral prospect, the warmer this first interaction will be.

The second factor is endorsement, either implied or explicit. In Section Four on prospecting for referrals, I will show you a sure-fire way to get your referral source to call your prospect before you call, to warm him or her up. This is an *explicit* endorsement. In an *implied* endorsement, you use the name of your referral source right away and mention that the referral was given because of the great service you provided.

Don't ever underestimate the power of commonality and endorsement. They are what turn a cold call into a warm call. They are what it takes these days to get past voice mail and all the other obstacles to selling. I've found that when I leave a voice-mail message from a cold call, it rarely gets returned. But when I leave a message from a referral, it usually gets returned.

Commonality and endorsement don't just make the first conversation easier. They also significantly increase the chance of the final sale. You'll get fewer obstacles and objections, you'll immediately operate from a higher level of trust, and your new prospect-turned-customer will have a stronger sense of loyalty right from the start.

Barry Graham Munro, in his book *Smart Salespeople Sometimes Wear Plaid* (Prima, 1994), says, "To some, a referral is merely a name. However, a referral is actually much more than this! A referral is the authorization to use the influence attached to that name."

Why don't all businesspeople build their business from referrals?

Quite frankly, this baffles me. Certainly, when you are first starting out in business, you have to make some cold calls to get the ball rolling. Certainly, some businesses lend themselves to referral selling more than others. But I've never run into a salesperson or business owner who can't use the methods I teach in this book.

I think part of the problem is that, until recently, there has been very little teaching in this area. In 1982, Tom Hopkins came out with *How to Master the Art of Selling* (Tom Hopkins International, 1982). Tom's techniques helped millions of salespeople become more effective. In his book, he calls referral prospecting the "backbone of prospecting for champions." Yet even he spends only a page and a half on the topic.

Dr. Ivan Misner has written a quality book called *The World's Best Known Marketing Secret: Building Your Business with Word-of-Mouth Marketing* (Bard & Stephen, 1994). He says, "Word-of-mouth marketing is a paradox. It is truly the world's best-known marketing secret." Practically everyone knows how important word-of-mouth is, yet very few people know how to develop it effectively.

Writes Misner, "For a phrase that is so universally recognized, it is amazing the concept is so little understood." Misner goes on to say that in many of the great marketing texts, word-of-mouth, like its close kin referrals, is barely addressed.

There are many salespeople, sales managers, and entrepreneurs who know how to generate tons of referrals. For the most part, these people have figured it out on their own. But there's no reason you need to figure it out all by yourself. I'm here to help you shorten your learning curve by years, maybe even decades.

A few books and speakers these days address this topic to some degree, and I will mention them throughout this book. You should know that, based on my extensive research in this area, you hold in your hands the most complete book to date on getting and using referrals. This book will give you the best of what others have shared, and a whole lot more.

I think it's time to elevate referral gathering to a new level of professionalism. Jay Abraham uses the phrase "ethical opportunism." Other people call it leverage. As you serve people better, and create relationships of trust, a little proactivity on your part will yield many opportunities for all parties, opportunities that go beyond the buyer/seller relationship.

Referral selling is a growing trend.

The use of referral is growing partly because of the obstacles I've already mentioned: voice mail (high tech, but low touch), increased competition, and everyone being busier than ever before.

However, it goes beyond these factors. You already know that our economy is fast becoming a service economy. Many salespeople are selling services instead of products. Those who are selling products are usually selling service to help distinguish their products from their competitors'. You can sell a product through literature, advertising, and cold calls. But it's much harder to sell a service that way. Service is a much less tangible sale. Buyers understand what good service is, but they can't hold it in their hands or watch it work before they buy it.

This is why meeting you through a colleague or friend is their preferred method. Your buyers would rather meet you through a referral. The endorsement and testimony of others make them feel much more comfortable opening their door to you and giving you their business.

The Foundation

Have the Right Attitude

Your Blueprint for Unlimited Referrals

In *Championship Selling* (MCJ Publishing, 1986), Marilyn Jennings writes, "The best prospect is the client who has already dealt with you. The second best is the one referred to you by a client who has dealt with you previously. The third best is one referred to you by another trusted professional or friend."

I've identified five critical steps to building a referral business. I'll use the metaphor of a house, or maybe I should think bigger and say "castle." Yes, a castle! A business that is big and strong, and less susceptible to negative influences.

The Foundation

Any great structure begins with a *foundation*. Your attitudes are the foundation of your sales castle. Your most important attitudes are a referral mindset and a desire to build relationships based on service and trust.

Your referral mindset

Having a referral mindset means that you have accepted the notion that the best way to build your business is by using referrals. Referrals are not just something nice that happens every now and then; they are your primary method for acquiring and selling new prospects. When you truly adopt a referral mindset, everything you do in the selling process will contribute to building your castle.

Relationships based on service

Once you have truly adopted your referral mindset, your referral business will prosper because of your ability to form quality relationships. You must enter into every relationship with an attitude of service. Throughout this book, I refer to the importance of relationships and service. Professional speaker and colleague Joe Bonura says, "Stop calling yourself a salesperson. Think of yourself as a serve person. You're not there to sell, but to serve." When you serve your prospects, your customers, and your referral alliances, the referrals (and the sales) will come easily. When you realize that using referrals is your most powerful strategy, that the relationships you form are crucial, and that these relationships grow because of your willingness to serve, you will have a rock-solid foundation upon which to place the four cornerstones.

You must enter into every relationship with an attitude of service.

The Four Cornerstones of a Referral Business

If you master any one of the four cornerstones, you'll be well on your way to increasing your business from unlimited referrals. If you master all four, you may never have to cold call again, and selling will be a consistently prosperous and pleasurable experience for you.

Here's a quick preview of the cornerstones, so you will have a general sense of what's ahead. Then we'll devote a section of the book to each one.

The first cornerstone: Exceed your customers' expectations

How do our customers say "thank you" to us? By coming back for more and by referring others to us. This is the first cornerstone, because without it, the other cornerstones would hardly be possible. You must serve your customers well continuously. Enough companies are providing such great service these days that the service you provide will be measured by what your customers know you are capable of.

Section Two of the book will give you some ideas and specific tools you can put to use immediately to make sure you are serving your customers so well that they are ready to refer more business your way.

In his classic *How to Sell Anything to Anybody* (Warner Books, 1977), Joe Girard says, "I look at every customer as if he is going to be like an *annuity* to me for the rest of my life. So they have to be happy. They have to believe in me."

The Guinness Book of World Records calls Joe Girard the world's greatest salesman. He claims to have sold more cars than anyone else, ever. He adds, "If you think the sale ends when, like they say in the car business, you see the customer's tail lights, you're going to lose more sales than you ever dreamed of. But if you understand how selling can be a continuing process that never ends, then you're going to make it to the big time."

Sometimes when I quote Joe Girard, people get nervous because they think I'm trying to turn them into the stereotypical car salesperson. Well, Joe isn't, nor am I. The methods I teach in this book can be used in the most sophisticated selling situations. You can adapt my techniques to your own situation.

The point is that the residual value of loyal customers is not just their return business over time, with better profits (although that's important). It's also their ability to connect you with who they know and who they can lead you to. Never forget that every customer has the ability to lead you to other customers.

The second cornerstone: Form referral alliances

Not all your referrals need come from satisfied customers. Many can come from the relationships you nurture with people who may never become customers. Section Three of this book will help you identify the people you already know who can give you a steady stream of referrals.

The key word with referral alliances is *service*. As you serve these people, they will serve you. As you help them become successful—with referrals, advice, or other help—they will refer people to you. One of the most powerful referrals a salesperson can receive is from another salesperson. So, quite often other salespeople will be your best referral alliances.

The third cornerstone: Prospect for referrals

In *Smart Salespeople Sometimes Wear Plaid,* Barry Graham Munro says that back in the 1800s, when people left their homes in search of gold, they became known as prospectors. "I guess this was because most of their time was spent searching for gold rather than actually finding it." In sales, too, only a small percentage of our time is actually engaged in the selling process. Most of us spend most of our time prospecting. Barry suggests, "Maybe we should call ourselves prospectors instead of salespeople! Of course, then we'd have to grow beards and everyone would want to see our mules. No, the title *salesperson* is fine, so long as we know that our real job is prospecting."

To achieve sustained success in selling, you must become a master prospector. Why prospect with cold calls when you can prospect for referrals? You'll spend more time in front of more qualified buyers, you'll make more sales, and you'll experience much less stress.

I'm really excited about this section of the book, because this is a topic about which very little has been written and taught to salespeople. Section Four will teach you how to raise your referral gathering to a whole new level of proactivity.

Many people are great at serving customers, because that's the "safe" side of sales. But these same salespeople don't know how to leverage those great relationships into a continuous flow of new referral prospects.

Read this section carefully. Apply the ideas and techniques to your specific situation as best you can, with a heavy dose of courage to try new ways. I guarantee you'll create more referrals than you ever thought possible.

The fourth cornerstone: Target niche markets

Creating a reputation for yourself and your company within one or more niches can substantially increase your referral business. When you target an industry, your requests for referrals are more targeted and therefore more effective. You also gain a high level of expertise, which will help you serve your prospects and customers better right from the start. You bring value to the first appointment that your competitors who don't target can't bring. You can engage in a deeper level of conversation right from the start.

> **Your reputation will spread much faster within a targeted group than it could between groups.**

Your reputation will spread much faster within a targeted group than it could between groups. Businesses in most industries tend to copy each other. When they find other businesses in their industry doing things that are working, they share the knowledge and help each other out. I know of one salesperson, Phil, who was introduced to more than 100 prospects by his happy customer. "How did he do it?" you might ask. Simple. The customer invited Phil to attend a trade show. He then walked up and down the aisles introducing Phil to everyone he knew.

Section Five will tell you everything you need to know to select and target niche markets. You will learn how to create such a reputation in your target industry that prospects will have heard great things about you before you even call.

Referrals will be gathered easily. In fact, many will seem to just come out of the blue. You'll experience a constant flow of found business.

You are on your way to an incredible new level of selling success!

I'd like to share a quote from another expert. In his book *Referrals* (Mark Sheer Seminars, 1993), Mark Sheer says, "A properly managed referral system will help you develop the ability to acquire more qualified appointments than you actually need. Why would you want more than you need? Because this will help you gain the competitive advantage over others in your field: the more qualified appointments you have, the more potential there will be for completed transactions. You will be in the enviable position of working only with people with whom you are compatible: people with whom you feel comfortable (doing business). You will no longer have to waste your time with people who are too time consuming, who drive you crazy, and who are just not any fun. You will have the liberty to be selective."

There are other books and tapes on the subject of referrals, but they cover only one of these cornerstones. This book will give you a comprehensive, step-by-step description of what you need to do and can do to significantly increase your sales by building your business based on referrals. Follow along with me now as I show you how to build your castle of unlimited referrals.

CHAPTER 2

The Relationship Is Everything

From the very first day I started selling, I knew intuitively that in sales, the relationships you establish with your prospects and with your customers are the basis for everything that gets accomplished. In my presentations to salespeople and business owners, I am always saying, "The relationship is everything!" As you begin to build your business from referrals, you must adopt the same attitude.

On the very first phone call to a prospect, it is the rapport you gain (the relationship) that allows the conversation to continue. It is the relationship that helps you feel more comfortable asking probing questions. It is the relationship that allows you to have a longer conversation than you expected. It is the quality of the relationship that develops that allows you to gain the appointment.

Work Toward a Partnership

On the appointment, it is the growing relationship that allows you to help clients reveal problems they are having. It is the relationship that allows you to find out with whom you are competing. It is the relationship that allows you to get a second appointment with more decision makers. It is the relationship that gets you invited to their planning meetings. Whatever you are selling, and whatever the sell cycle, it is the relationship you establish that gives you influence with your prospect.

Once your prospect becomes a customer, the better the relationship you can achieve, the more you have a true partnership rather than just a buyer/seller situation.

Don't be a vendor or supplier

I hate the words *vendor* and *supplier.* Unless you are dealing with a purchasing agent who insists on using those words, I suggest you expunge them from your vocabulary. I prefer the word *partnership.* A partner is always interested in creating win/win situations, where in every transaction both the buyer and the seller win.

Practice Relationship Selling

From my very first day in sales, with every prospect I encountered, I worked to establish a relationship of mutual trust. I worked to create business friends. Then I read a great book by Jim Cathcart entitled *Relationship Selling* (Perigee Books, 1990). This book confirmed all I had figured out on my own, and then some.

Jim Cathcart's philosophy on relationship selling is fundamental to what I will teach you in this book. Without good relationships with prospects, customers, and referral alliances, you cannot create unlimited referrals. I like to think of my *referral selling* methods as the next step beyond Jim's *relationship selling.* Without quality relationships, referral selling won't work. Once you have quality relationships, it's time to leverage them into referrals.

When I called Jim Cathcart and asked for permission to explain his work, he asked me to emphasize that relationship selling is not just staying in touch with a prospect or customer. Relationship selling is not just a series of techniques. "It's a philosophy," he said, "a way of doing business."

Referral selling is also more than just a series of techniques. Referral selling is a philosophy, a way of doing business, a mindset that has relationship selling at its core. Create relationships, create true business friendships, and each side of the partnership will continually work to serve the other.

Cathcart observes that all good salespeople have two traits in common. First, they love to make sales. In fact, they thrive on it. Second, and of equal importance, they respect their prospects and customers. These two qualities are the keys to success in *relationship selling*. "Selling should be a friendly act. Something we do to help people. Something we do *with* people and *for* people, not *to* them," says Jim.

A new way to sell

Although most salespeople have changed with the times and have moved away from the old style of *adversary selling*, there are still remnants that show up in the language of sales. An example is the verb *close*. We use this word liberally to mean the completing of a sale. But is it really a close? Close implies an ending. And it implies something that we do *to* people rather than *for* them. What we are really trying to do is *confirm* the sale, confirm the relationship, confirm the beginning of a partnership.

Traditional selling was characterized by catchphrases like: Selling is a contest, selling is persuading, customers must be sold, buyers are liars, and the close is #1. These attitudes worked—but usually only once with each buyer. Contrast this with relationship selling: Selling is service, selling is helping, customers love to buy, buyers want a salesperson they can trust, and follow-through is #1.

Manage the tension in the sale

One of the biggest obstacles to effective selling is tension between the buyer and the seller. Managing and controlling the tension level is one of the best ways a seller can increase the likelihood of a sale. When the tension is up, cooperation is down. When the tension is down, trust and cooperation begin to rise.

When you first contact most prospects, the tension level is high. They don't know who you are or why you are calling. They've probably had bad experiences with pushy salespeople. So you get a knee-jerk reaction that's not always pleasant.

When you get together on an appointment, the buyers' tension level can continue to be high, because they want to make sure they make the decision to buy, and aren't sold. Your tension level starts to go up at this phase because you now have more at stake.

The tension level will ease a bit for both parties as you explore the relationship potential. But as the confirming stage draws near, if the tension has not been managed well it will certainly increase for you, and probably for the buyer as well.

One of the biggest obstacles to effective selling is tension between the buyer and the seller.

So, how do you keep the tension level low? Cathcart argues that "behavioral flexibility" is the key: your ability to adapt your own behavior so that your prospect feels more comfortable. This is not manipulation. You are merely giving your prospect the gift of your flexibility, so he or she will feel more comfortable. Sales expert Tony Alessandra calls this the platinum rule. "Do unto others as they would like to be done unto." Treat people the way they want to be treated, and sell to them the way they want to be sold.

Here's the rule of thumb that I go by: *The way people communicate to you is the way they best hear your words.* If someone is very direct in his or her communication, then I know I need to be more direct. But if someone is less direct, softer in approach, I must soften up. If customers are more open than I am, I know I need to give them more time to talk and to handle relationship stuff before I get down to business. If they are more contained than I am, I need to adjust my expectations. They will have less to say and will let me into their life at a slower pace than I might prefer.

There is a term in biology that sums all this up perfectly: *requisite variety.* It means that in any given ecosystem, organisms with the widest range of responses thrive the most. Salespeople with the widest range of responses to people who come into their lives are the ones who thrive.

Mediocre salespeople sell the same way to everyone. Given enough time, they'll probably find enough people who want to buy that way and will achieve moderate success. But good salespeople are naturally flexible with the people they meet. They instinctively adjust their communications, expectations, and behavior to build rapport. Great salespeople have superior awareness when it comes to flexibility. They consciously adjust their communications, expectations, and behavior to help the prospect feel more comfortable and establish a win/win situation.

Of course, selling from referrals reduces tension for you and your prospect right from the start.

The Five Keys to Creating Influence for Win/Win Results

In a program entitled *Creating Influence,* I share my five keys for achieving influence. I give them to you now, because they support the philosophy of *relationship selling:* Lasting influence can be created only when you attend to the relationship first.

1. **Awareness.** You must be aware of who you are, your style of communication, how you process information, what your priorities are, and the speed at which you move through life. Then you must become aware of others and how they differ from you.

2. **Empathy.** Once you've gained greater awareness, you are in a position to feel empathy for others. You can "walk in their shoes" for a while and figure out what's important to them, how they differ from you, and how they are similar—and do all of this *without judging them!*

33

3. Benefits. You must communicate the benefits to them if you expect to have any lasting influence. Figure out what's in it for them, help them create a win for themselves (that is also a win for you), and you've created influence. Now you can solve a problem or take advantage of an opportunity.

4. Flexibility. You must be willing to make the first move. You will earn no influence with others just by wishing. You must first be willing to adjust *your* behavior to affect *their* behavior.

5. Courage. It can take great courage to get more in touch with yourself and with others. It can take great courage to adjust your behavior, not knowing if it will make any difference. It takes great courage to create relationships built on honesty, trust, and clear communication.

This is merely a glimpse into the philosophy of relationship selling—with my added editorial. Jim Cathcart's *Relationship Selling* is a landmark book that changed the way thousands of salespeople sell. I urge you to purchase a copy. Once you master the philosophy of *relationship selling*, you can begin to achieve lasting success in sales. Then you can experience the next level of success as you begin to use my principles of *referral selling*.

CHAPTER 3

Listening: The Greatest Relationship Builder

W e live in a society of poor listeners. Unfortunately, most salespeople fall into this category. We never learned how to listen. Even though well over half of human communication occurs through listening, we don't receive any training in this area. We are taught how to read, write, and speak, but rarely how to listen. The most my teachers in school ever said about listening was, "Class. Listen!"

But *listening* is the most important relationship skill you can practice. It's a relationship skill because everyone needs to be listened to. Everyone! And when you listen to someone actively, with good focus, that person can feel it. To build trust and rapport with prospects, customers, and referral alliances, listen well.

In addition to its relationship-building properties, listening helps you learn about your prospects, customers, and referral alliances so you'll be in a stronger position to serve them. In later chapters, I will explain how listening to your customers puts you in a position to create many more win/win situations. Without good listening habits, you will miss many opportunities to serve them, and yourself.

Learn to Manage Your Distractions

Becoming a focused and active listener is mostly a matter of managing the distractions. External distractions are things such as noise, the phone ringing, a pretty woman or handsome man walking by, and interruptions in all their varieties. Internal distractions are things such as preparing your response while the other party is still speaking, shutting down because you disagree with what the person is saying, and being preoccupied with judging the speaker based on his or her style or accent or clothing.

People usually talk at about 100 to 120 words per minute. But you can think at 400 to 600 words per minute. So, even if you are paying close attention, you still have tons of free time in your head. How you manage that free time will determine the quality of your listening, and ultimately the quality of the relationships you establish.

Become an Active Listener

Dr. Tony Alessandra is a colleague of mine who is a fantastic and successful speaker. He has authored numerous books and tapes, including *The Dynamics of Effective Listening, The Platinum Rule,* and *Non-Manipulative Selling.* Tony says there are three types of listening dynamics: marginal, evaluative, and active listening.

Marginal listening

Marginal listeners may be guilty of:

- Being preoccupied with their own thoughts or feelings.
- Distracting the speaker with nervous mannerisms.
- Conveying a self-centered, arrogant attitude.
- Misunderstanding much of what has been said.
- Not even hearing what has been said.

Here's an example of marginal listening:

Customer:
> You want me to take a whole day off from work so I can sit at home *all day* waiting for your repairman to show up?

Customer Service Rep:
> Our first available day is two weeks from Monday.
>
> (Meanwhile, the CSR is thinking, "Just a half-hour to go before lunch.")

Evaluative listening

Although better than marginal listeners, evaluative listeners still are not fully present. They are guilty of:

- Categorizing or evaluating what is said rather than trying to listen and understand.
- Concentrating on composing a response.
- Making quick judgments about the speaker.
- Finishing the speaker's sentences.
- Getting distracted by emotionally loaded words.
- Rushing through the conversation.

Evaluative listening sounds something like this:

Customer:
> You want me to take a whole day off from work so I can sit at home *all day* waiting for your repairman to show up?

Customer Service Rep (defensively):
> This is our busiest time of the year and there's nothing I can do about it.

Active listening

Active listening takes desire and effort on your part. Active listeners:

- Concentrate on what people are saying.
- Control their impulse to finish people's sentences. (They are patient listeners.)
- Make an effort to see the speaker's point of view. (They listen with empathy.)
- Give feedback to the speaker.

Active listening leads to a sincere response like this:

Customer:

You want me to take a whole day off from work so I can sit at home *all day* waiting for your repairman to show up?

Customer Service Rep:

I can see that would be a major inconvenience for you. Unfortunately, this is our busiest time of the year and qualified technicians are hard to come by. Could you arrange for a neighbor to let our service person in?

It isn't enough to listen actively. We must *show* the speaker that we are listening. If we don't make that effort, the relationship value of our listening will be lost.

Active, focused listening is part of your attitude of service. It's a gift you give to others so that they will feel more comfortable with you. It's a gift that will pay you back many times over.

Demonstrate That You Are Listening

There are many effective ways to show that you are paying attention and encourage the speaker to tell you more.

- Use your body language to show interest and energy. Lean forward or put your hand on your chin. Make good eye contact (but don't stare down the speaker).

- Ask questions that relate to what they are saying.

- Repeat back in your words (paraphrase) what they've said to ensure understanding.

- Over the phone, vocally acknowledge with "uh-huh," "yeah," or "mmm" every 15 to 20 seconds so they know you're listening.

- Take notes.

- Don't interrupt.

- Don't clip the ends of their sentences.

- Acknowledge what they've said before changing direction in the conversation.

The First Cornerstone

Exceed Your Customers' Expectations

CHAPTER 4

Create Legendary Service

Referral selling begins with great customer service—service so good that your customers want to tell others. The higher the level of service you provide to your customers, the more willing they are to give you high-quality referrals.

The bottom line of providing great service is that you must care about your customers, and you must care about giving great service. You must want to do it. You must have an *attitude of service* with your customers. An attitude of service is almost impossible to teach. Either you have it or you don't. For referral selling to work for you, you must develop your attitude of service.

Shep Hyken says in *Moments of Magic: Be a Star with Your Customers and Keep Them Forever* (The Alan Press, 1993), "Going the extra mile does not necessarily mean a lot of extra effort. It just requires caring and thinking about the needs of your customers; knowing *your* business and anticipating *their* needs and potential problems."

Your customers are happy when you meet their expectations of your product and service. Your customers are loyal and become "word-of-mouth machines" when you exceed their expectations. Serve your customers well and they will serve you well!

Exceed Expectations

A simple example of exceeding customer expectations happened to me while in the middle of writing this book. Over one weekend, while doing some work on my house and yard, I had to patronize three large do-it-yourself home centers. In each case I was in a hurry, so I stopped a floor person (I hesitate to call them sales or customer service people) for assistance. What did I expect? I expected them to politely tell me exactly where the item that I wanted was located.

At the first store, the floor person wasn't quite sure of the answer, so he gave me some vague point and mumble. This didn't meet my expectations, and I left with a bad feeling about the store.

At the second store, the floor person pointed to the aisle and said, "It should be somewhere on aisle D. If it's not there, try the end of aisle E." Then he went on his way. This was better, but I still had to wander around for a long time before I found the item—at the end of aisle F.

At the third store (this is beginning to remind me of the three little pigs and the big bad wolf) not only did the floor person know exactly where the item was, but also he stopped what he was doing and took me to the spot. This exceeded my expectations. I was a happy wolf. Now I shop there most often, even going out of my way on occasion.

Margaret is a financial advisor with American Express Financial Advisors. Margaret truly has an attitude of service. Whenever she refers a client to another professional, such as an accountant or attorney, she accompanies the client to the first meeting. Her attitude of service has paid off; Margaret is a top producer.

What Do Your Customers Expect?

To exceed your customers' expectations as often as possible, you have to know what those expectations are. Do you ask your prospects and customers what great service means to them and what it will take to make them happy? Do you ask them why they went with your company? Why they left the company that served them previously? What it takes to keep them happy, and what it takes to make them lose confidence? If you aren't having this type of conversation with your customers, then you're not serving them, or yourself, very well.

To exceed their expectations, you must first know what those expectations are. If you make the effort to find out, they will appreciate it, you will stand out from the others, and you will be in a better position to serve your customers so well that they start to refer you to others. You will have what I like to call positional advantage (advantage over the competition).

> **Serve your customers so well that they talk about you to others.**

In her book *Serving Them Right: Innovative and Powerful Customer Retention Strategies* (Harper Business, 1990), Laura Liswood points out, "It is important to remember that people's perceptions and expectations are constantly changing. As customers move from one buying experience to another, they are exposed to different types and levels of service, and their future expectations will typically be based upon the best experience they've had in the past. This means the best in any circumstance, regardless of the type of merchandise or service involved."

A phrase I heard recently perfectly describes what we're talking about here: "Create legendary service." You must create legendary customer service, service so good that customers talk about it to others. Your customers can be part of your sales force, and you don't have to pay them any commission. You just have to wow them as often as you can.

The Human-Business Model

In her book *Building Customer Loyalty* (Irwin Professional Publishing, 1994), Barbara Glanz explains a helpful distinction she calls the human-business model that was created by Kaset International (a customer service training company headquartered in Tampa, Florida). "In every interaction we have, something is happening simultaneously on two levels, the human level and the business level. The business level gets the work done while the human level is all about how the participant feels about the interaction. The customer's experience is the combined result of both the business and the human levels of the interactions. Customers want their business needs met (after all, that is why they seek and pay for the product or service), while being treated with respect, friendliness, and empathy."

Let's say you go into a discount appliance store to buy a new television. You find the model you want at the price you want, but the salesperson is a little obnoxious and not very helpful. Do you buy the TV? Probably. Do you refer other people to the store? Maybe. Do you refer others to that sales-person? Definitely not.

Sometimes the human side of the equation won't prevent the sale. But, more often than not, it will decrease the likelihood of repeat business and kill the possibility of referrals.

Glanz makes another helpful distinction between what she calls core service and customer service. "Core service is the service or product your organization or work team provides to its customers, the business you are in, or your 'reason for being.' Your organization or team would have no purpose without this core service.

"Customer service is the delivery system of the product or service—how the customers are *treated* in the interactions they have while conducting the business. It includes both the people involved as well as the processes that are used (policies, practices, procedures)."

Glanz says that customers want four things:

1. Friendly, caring service. Customers want to be treated with courtesy and respect. They want to feel that *they* are important.

2. Flexibility. Customers want you to jiggle the system for them and their individual needs. They

don't want to hear no; they want you to figure out a way to get them what they want or need.

3. Problem solving. Customers want the first person they speak to to solve their problem, not the supervisor or manager.

4. Recovery. When the organization or the employee has made a mistake, customers want them to apologize, fix the mistake, do something extra, and follow up. They want to be taken care of quickly and to their satisfaction.

It's critical that you deliver quality on both accounts, core service and customer service. Fall down on either and you'll lose customers as fast as you acquire them.

Glanz suggests that the core service works to *meet* the customer's expectations, and the customer service works to *exceed* expectations and create customer loyalty. In her words, "Core service and customer service have different objectives. The goal of core service is to *satisfy* the customer, while the goal of customer service is to *dazzle* (delight or surprise) the customer. Core service first attracts a customer to an organization, and extraordinary customer service keeps a customer returning."

To deliver service that is legendary—service that makes your customers want to help you grow your business by giving you referrals—you must deliver quality core service and dazzling customer service. People refer business to people they like and trust. The best referrals usually come from truly loyal customers. In this section of the book, I will give you some of the ingredients of legendary service. Incorporate these ideas and strategies into your everyday actions and your customers will grow to like and trust you. And you will be well on your way to building your referral business.

Your Commitment to Service

Your attitude of service becomes a commitment to service when you put it into action. Are you truly committed to your career as a professional salesperson or entrepreneur? Then customer retention must be among your top priorities. Harvey Mackay, author of *Swim With The Sharks Without Being Eaten Alive* (Morrow, 1988), writes, "It's one thing to get the first order . . . it's quite another thing to get the re-order." If you're not getting re-orders, then you're not creating a situation in which you can successfully collect referrals.

Turn Your Attitude into Action

Almost every business has a repurchase cycle. Most people buy a new car within three to five years, a new copier every two to three years, a new computer every two to three years, and so on. Cycles vary, but most industries have one. Yours may be less frequent, or much more frequent.

If you've sold someone an item to give as a birthday or anniversary gift, then about 330 days later, you want to call them for the next opportunity. If you served them well the first time and did a little follow-up throughout the year, then your call will be well received, even appreciated.

The point is that if you are in it for the long haul, you will do what it takes to make sure that customer buys from you next time. Most truly successful salespeople depend on repeat business to sustain their success over many years.

If this is what you want for yourself, keep reading. If you're only in it for a few years, to make a few quick sales, then put this book down now, because these ideas won't mean much to you.

Your Integrity Will Be Tested

In business, integrity means at least two things. First, it means doing what you say you'll do. Second, it means never violating your own standards of behavior.

Every time you tell a customer (or prospect) that you will do something, you'd better do it. This is how trust is built. Let your customers know from the very beginning that your word means something. Show them they can count on you to do what you say you will.

This is not always an easy standard to uphold. Often we agree to something without thinking it all the way through, only to realize later that we misjudged our ability to deliver on our promise.

There are two ways to avoid this problem.

1. Be careful what you say you will do. Be thoughtful with how you give your word. Take an extra moment to look at your schedule or think through the situation. My customers have become accustomed to my making careful decisions. And since I follow through on my word, they appreciate my thoughtfulness. Robert Schuller says, "Those who fail, fail to follow through." If you say you will have a project done by 4 P.M. Monday, get it done. If there is a good reason why it won't be done by then, don't wait for the customer to call you. Call him as soon as you know you won't be on time. Keeping promises is essential to maintaining your integrity and building trust.

2. If you do make an error in judgment, tell your customer immediately. If you tell a customer you'll have

something ready at a certain time and later you realize that was a poor decision, call him immediately. I can guarantee that if time passes and you don't call, he will remember it. And even if he forgives you later, he'll withhold his trust until you prove yourself all over again.

The second aspect of integrity has to do with your word to yourself. A person with integrity never engages in behavior that goes against his or her own standards. Your customers will respect and trust you when they see that you have high standards for yourself, even when that means not giving them exactly what they want.

Don't get me wrong; you need to be infinitely flexible in how you serve your customers. No service policy should be written in stone. But your personal standards should never be violated. True, you may lose a customer now and then who asks you to do business in a way that violates your personal standards. But compromising on what you hold important does not allow for a win/win selling situation. Every sale must be a win for both you and the customer. Customers who don't let you have your half of the equation are not good customers.

Setting your personal standards for business (and the rest of your life) is an ongoing process. Sometimes we aren't even aware of a standard until it is tested. It's a process worth your thought and energy.

Integrity is your foundation for creating trust with your customers, not to mention everyone else in your life. When people talk about you behind your back, you want them to say, "I can count on her," or "He's a man of his word."

Following are some steps you can take to demonstrate your integrity and commitment to service.

Tell the truth

Never lie to a customer. Keeping track of the truth is hard enough. With that said, *when* to tell the truth in certain businesses is something of an art form. Situations may come up in which the customer does not need to know every detail all at once. However, make it a general policy to tell the truth to your customers.

Thank your customers often

Almost every salesperson I meet knows about the value of sending a thank-you note after making a sale or performing a service. Yet most salespeople are not in the habit of doing this. This gesture alone will help you to stand out from most of the salespeople who call on your customers.

A handwritten note is good. I have such bad hand-writing that I use my computer, but I make sure they can tell that this is a personal thanks, just for them, and not a form letter.

Shep Hyken *(Moments of Magic)* tells the story of a cab driver he uses every time he travels to Dallas. The first time Shep rode with him, this driver explained some of the sights along the way. Then, Shep writes, "He asked for my business card. He said he collects the business cards of the people he drives. The fare was $22, but I paid him $30 to give him a nice tip. It was a great ride. *A moment of magic.*

"Four days later, I was in my office in St. Louis. I opened my mail and found a thank-you note from my cab driver, Frank Nelson. I was overwhelmed and shocked. The note read, 'I thank you for the opportunity to take you from the convention center to the airport. I hope you enjoyed the fountain.' That thank-you note made my day . . . actually it made my week! How many times have you received a thank-you note from your cab driver?

"Now, when I go to Dallas, I call Frank. Frank picks me up at the airport and takes me anywhere I want to go. I have told others about him. While working a convention in Dallas, I gave his name to three clients, and they used him.

"Then, Christmas time came. What do I get in the mail from Frank Nelson? A Christmas card!

"Frank Nelson treats his customers just the way he would want to be treated. His theory is that by doing this he will make more money than any other cab driver in Dallas.

"He is absolutely right! He does!"

Show your appreciation

You can show you appreciate your customers in many other ways besides thank-you notes.

Many people like to keep a steady stream of ad specialties flowing to their customers: mugs, pens, sticky-notes, and the like. I suggest you look for even more creative ways to use ad specialties as part of your appreciation mix.

I know of one company that sends inspirational poems mounted in walnut frames to their customers at Thanksgiving. As they count their blessings, their customers are among them.

Can you hold a really neat social event for your customers? Treat them to something special to show your appreciation. You might suggest they invite their colleagues (possible referrals for you).

What added service or special discounts can you give to your most valued customers? Perhaps you could create a special "frequent customer" discount or special reward.

If you aren't your company's top executive, persuade her to visit some of your most valued customers, just to reinforce your entire company's appreciation of their business. Have her bring along a thank-you card signed by many of the employees.

Create superior internal customer service

You already know that you have external customers (or clients). Have you thought about who your *internal* customers are? Include everyone in your organization who has a role in helping you serve your external customers.

These folks are *your* customers because they deliver goods, services, or information to you so that you can deliver to your external customer. You are *their* customer because you have to deliver information to them so that they can do their job most efficiently and effectively.

Barbara Glanz says, "It is a lot easier to create loyal external customers if the organization's internal customers are cared for and supported. Research shows that the way an organization's internal customers are treated is ultimately the way the external customer will be treated.

"Employee loyalty also has an impact on customer loyalty. Have you ever been in an organization where people really seemed to enjoy their work? Chances are they are well treated as internal customers, and this makes them feel good and makes them better able to serve the external customer as well."

So, consider these questions: Have you (and your company) identified all your internal customers? Do you sit down together on a regular basis to discuss how you can serve each other better so your external customers are served impeccably?

Clarify—don't assume!

When customers give you "fuzzy phrases," make sure you are on the same wavelength. Don't leave room for misunderstandings. When customers say they need something "as soon as possible," stop and find out exactly what that means to them.

Record every service transaction

Most effective salespeople document their prospecting efforts. They keep track of each contact and each conversation. However, most salespeople stop there. They don't usually keep good documentation going once the sale has been made.

I know a sales rep for a building contractor who uses his laptop computer to keep a running log of every job. Every time something happens, he puts it into this temporary document. Once the job is completed, he prints it out and then erases it from the computer. This helps him keep track of the job and comes in handy if a problem arises later.

How can you apply this idea to your serving situation?

Never call a customer wrong

We all know the customer is not always right. But we have to be very careful how we let *them* know that.

I once took some negatives to a photo lab to be turned into prints. It was about 20 different negatives, so the order was a little complicated. I read off the numbers I wanted printed to the store clerk and she recorded them. When she read the order back to me, it was not what I had wanted. She immediately told me, in an accusatory tone, that I had given her the wrong numbers. Of course, I became mildly angry.

The truth of the matter is that I may have made a mistake. We'll never know for sure. But when she accused me of the error, she damaged her and the lab's relationship with me. I may go back to that lab in spite of her, but certainly not because of her.

Be very careful how you let customers know they've made a mistake. Take as much on yourself as possible first. And when you do have to tell them, do it in a teaching manner—not arrogantly or patronizingly, but from a place of genuine care and concern.

CHAPTER 6

How to Exceed Expectations

There are many things you can do to exceed your customers' expectations and create legendary service. Here are some time-tested ideas. Use as many as you can. Exceeding expectations is a function of your desire and your creativity. Be creative in how you serve your customers, and they will spread the word to others.

Call Customers with Status Reports

Depending on your business, you may have opportunities to call your customers between the time they place the order and when you deliver it. Schedule one or more status report calls to let your customers know that everything is on schedule. They will appreciate you, checking on their order or project. And everyone appreciates a "good news" call.

Always "Install" Your Product

In *Relationship Selling,* Jim Cathcart says, "The most successful salespeople don't just sell their product or service, they *install* it after the sale. No matter what your line of business, devise a way to make your client feel comfortable with the product or service after the sale." Cathcart offers the following examples for installing a product or service:

1. If you sell residential real estate, give each buyer an owner's manual for the new home. Show buyers where the gas, water, and electric switches and meters are. Prepare a list of important phone numbers for their neighborhood. Give them a map that shows nearby schools, churches, and stores.

2. If you sell automobiles, take time to show the buyer how to operate the new car. Go over the manufacturer's manual, and be willing to answer questions.

3. If your product is clothing, show the customer how to use accessories with it to create a different look.

4. If you sell insurance, prepare a summary emphasizing that this wasn't a one-time purchase and that as their insurance needs changes over the years, you'll be there to provide guidance and to suggest the right policy.

"The key to continued success," Cathcart concludes, "is showing the customer how to maximize the use of whatever was purchased."

If you sell an ongoing service such as printing, bookkeeping, or temporary employment services, introduce customers to people in your office with whom they are likely to come into contact. Your customers will be more comfortable and trusting each time they call a member of your team.

My speaking and writing business has been good to me. Recently, I felt lucky to be able to afford a brand new Lexus automobile. The whole experience was like nothing I've ever experienced before from a car dealer. In fact, one of the reasons I finally decided on the Lexus was that every time I walked into a Lexus dealership I was treated with great care and respect. It was a breath of fresh air compared with the "games" I've experienced at many other dealerships.

My Lexus salesperson did just what I've discussed. After the sale, he introduced me to the service manager and a few other people with whom I might have contact. As my car was brought around for me to drive home, he carefully went through almost every detail of the car to make sure I would get the most pleasure from it. He even had a small but classy gift for me. Whenever I take the car in for service or the free car wash, my salesperson and his colleagues take a moment to see how I and my car are doing.

I've already referred several people to that dealership. This shows how important the after-the-sale phase is, especially if you want your customers to give you referrals.

Be Careful How You Turn Customers Over to Customer Service

First of all, it's my feeling that everyone in your company is part of your "customer service" department. Everyone should be ready, willing, and able to speak to customers and satisfy their needs as best they can.

Since every customer has the potential to lead many more customers to you, you should always welcome opportunities to serve them—long after the sale has been made. Even if your company has a customer service department, be careful how you turn your customers over to it.

Several months ago I switched my long-distance telephone service to a small company that had great rates. The salesperson was great at showing me how I'd benefit from his service. I was happy with the prices he quoted and with his initial service. So, when he asked me for referrals, I gave him three.

A month later, I began to have problems with the calling-card feature of the service. When I called the salesperson, he acted as if he couldn't be bothered and said that I needed to talk to "customer service."

This left me feeling burned. I'll never recommend this service to anyone else, because the salesperson betrayed my trust. And since the problem hasn't been resolved yet, I'm about to switch my service again.

Maintain Good Relationships with Your Vendors

Karin Collis is the owner of Karin's Custom Images, an ad specialty business. She says, "In this business, normal production time is four to six weeks. But I've built relationships with factories that meet rush demands. A customer may call me in desperation because he needs something for a trade show in a few days. Because of the relationships I've nurtured, I can usually find something and have it in his hands the day he needs it."

Find other companies who will help you be a hero to your customers.

Know Your Competition

When you know your competition well, it not only gives you a selling advantage early on but also continues to help you serve and sell to your customer throughout the relationship.

You should always serve your customers with the knowledge that they are under pressure to move their business elsewhere. The pressure may be internal, though more likely it's external, from all the other salespeople calling on them every day.

Do you know what pressures your customers are under to move their business? Do you know what they say to all those other salespeople? If you don't, I suggest you get to know your customers better and find out. The more you know about your competition, the more you can do to make sure you are better than they are.

Your customers may also use one or more of your competitors. When you take your customers' satisfaction temperatures, find out what those competitors are doing well, and learn and improve from them. Find out what your competitors aren't doing so well, and learn from their mistakes.

Get to Know Your Customers

Whenever possible, get to know your customers beyond just the buying-selling-serving relationship. Get to know them as people. Take a genuine interest in them. Not every customer wants you to do this, but most will appreciate it.

The customers who give me the best referrals and continue to give me referrals long after I've served them are those I now count as friends. If your attitude is strictly business, you are probably missing tons of opportunities for referrals, not to mention more business from your existing customers.

Getting to know your customers better helps to create stronger loyalty. And the more you know them as human beings, the more you'll be able to exceed their expectations.

In *Swim With the Sharks*, Harvey Mackay tells about a selling tool he and his salespeople have been using for years. He calls it the "Mackay 66" because it's 66 questions about your customers. If you know the answers to them all, you have great customer relationships. Collecting this kind of information leads you to deeper relationships and helps you serve your customers better.

> "It is the service we are not obliged to give that people value the most."
>
> J.C. Penney

Besides the standard stuff such as their spouses' and children's names and birthdays, the Mackay 66 asks about customers' educational background, business history, and lifestyle. (For example, favorite foods, favorite places for lunch and dinner, hobbies, vacation habits, and sports interests.) The list also asks, "Whom does the customer seem anxious to impress?"

This is not a list of questions that you put in front of your customers. It is your very private list that you keep lively in your awareness. I highly recommend that you get a copy of *Swim With the Sharks* and check out the Mackay 66. Either use Mackay's list or create your own. The important thing is that you have a tool that will help you deepen your relationships.

Guess why golf is such a popular tool for doing business in America? It's because people get to know each other in ways other than the buying-selling-servicing relationship. If you don't play golf now . . . don't start! It's much too humbling a game. (I'm just kidding. I've just started playing, after all these years. I've taken some lessons that have made a huge difference. And guess what? I'm using it to develop stronger relationships with customers and prospects.)

Get to Know Your Customers' Companies

Get to know your clients in ways that go beyond what you sell. Find out what their goals are. Find out what problems they are having in areas that, at first glance, have little or nothing to do with what you sell. This will help you serve them in many ways over time. You will become a much more valuable resource and can even occasionally provide them with other resources.

If you sell printing and you view yourself as merely a vendor or supplier, you may never get to know your customers well. If you see yourself as a partner who is not just selling print services but is also helping them communicate information, then you will get to know them much more deeply, and you will be in a position to create many more win/win situations.

Help Your Customers Really Know Your Company

Don't get pigeonholed. Your customers first started doing business with you based on their need at the time. Even though you told them about the full range of what you offer, all they probably saw was the specific product or service that would help them with that specific need.

You serve your customers better when you keep them informed of everything you offer. If you sold them life insurance, make sure they also know you handle disability insurance and other financial services. If you sold them two-color printing, make sure they know you do four-color as well.

If you've created a good working relationship, customers will thank you for reminding them of other ways you can help make their life easier.

Find Ways to Compliment Your Customers

I like to buy nice suits at a great price. I shop in a little store that is attached to the factory where the suits are made. If I don't like anything hanging on the rack, the salesperson will go into the plant to see what's being worked on that day.

Because this factory is more than an hour from my home, I take the suits to a local tailor to have them fitted. The last time I bought a suit this way, I was reminded of the value of complimenting the customer in any way you can.

I was trying on the suit. As the tailor, an elderly Italian gentleman, measured he said, "This a nice suit. Where you get-a this suit?"

I told him.

"This a nice suit. I gonna take-a my time with this suit."

I felt great. I'd thought I was getting a nice suit, and now my opinion was validated by an Italian tailor.

A week later, I went in to pick up the suit. I tried it on. He moved it around a little. Then he said, "This a nice suit. Where you get-a this suit?"

I told him.

"This a nice suit. I took-a my time with this suit."

I felt great again. Maybe he says this to everyone, but maybe not. He liked my suit. I liked him. That's the way this concept works.

Become an Expert in Your Field

"Knowledge of our business is vital," Shep Hyken says in *Moments of Magic.* "We never stop learning. We must continually read and study to keep abreast of new developments. When you become an expert in your field, you will gain the respect of your customers, both on the outside and within your organization. You will be looked upon as a source for information.

"Why are consultants constantly writing articles and giving seminars? They want to share their expertise and position themselves as experts.

"Present yourself as an expert and offer to be a source of information. Customers will come to respect you, and will be more likely to come to you for business.

"How can you become an expert? Noted speaker Brian Tracy says if you read on a subject for an hour each day, within two to three years you will become an expert. If you continue to read on for an hour a day over three to five years, you will become an authority. After five to seven years, you will be an international authority. He adds that if you read just one book a month you will join the top one percent of the population."

Keep Serving Your Customers After the Sale

Since you know that every customer you serve is connected to other potential customers, you want to keep finding opportunities to serve them, even in ways that have nothing to do with what you sell.

Lynne Schwabe, a marketing consultant, tells a story that illustrates this point perfectly. "After completing a project for Client A in San Francisco, I provided something extra by sending him a list of resources directly related to his additional needs. He was so appreciative of the extra service I gave him that he referred me to Client B in Atlanta, who referred me to Clients C and D. Client C has referred me to Client E in Denver and Client F in Galveston, Texas. This is the story that never ends." As well it shouldn't, I might add.

By doing a little something extra for one client, Lynne created a chain reaction that may never stop. That's the power of great service coupled with the attitude of working from referrals. The result: unlimited referrals.

Create a Useful Customer Survey

You should be constantly asking your customers, "How am I doing?" "If we could do one thing better, what would it be?" And you should be asking these questions face to face (over the phone is second best).

But a formal survey of customers can also have its place. Many customers feel more comfortable giving candid feedback if it's through a written survey. I suggest that this survey come from management so that it can compile candid information about the salesperson. Very few salespeople want to hear what their customers really think–but they should. Look at the survey as a good friend who is willing to tell you the truth, no matter what, to help you get rid of unproductive habits in favor of more productive ones.

In *Beware the Naked Man Who Offers You His Shirt* (Morrow, 1990) Harvey Mackay reprints the customer survey he uses at Mackay Envelope Corp. This is a fun book to read, full of great information. The customer survey alone is worth the investment.

Sometimes the Little Things Are the Big Things

Customers for Life: How to Turn That One-Time Buyer into a Lifetime Customer (Doubleday, 1990), by Carl Sewell and Paul Brown, is a well-known book on customer service. It contains many great ideas and strategies. At the end of each chapter is a checklist of specifics that nearly everyone should be doing with and for customers. With permission from the publisher, I have selected some of these specifics to share with you (along with my comments). Do you have this attitude of service? Are you doing these things as a matter of habit? My commentary is in italics.

- **Stretch.** You cut lawns for a living, and your customer needs the name of a good tree surgeon? Find him one. If he is staying at your hotel and his car gets a flat, change it. Help your customer.

- **Don't charge for this "extra" service if you can help it.** If it's something that a friend would do for another friend, don't charge. Don't worry, you'll more than make up the money in future business. *And referrals.*

- **You can't just provide good service between 9 A.M. and 5 P.M.** If you're going to provide good service, you have to provide it around the clock. *Give them your home phone number. They may never use it, but it reassures them.*

- **Talk about the mistakes.** Log every single job that is brought back. As soon as it comes in, fix it. Then find out how the problem was able to slip through in the first place.

- **Keep the service promise.** Doing what you're supposed to do, when you are supposed to do it, is the very minimum required to provide good customer service.

- **When something goes wrong** and it will, no matter how hard you try, **apologize.** It's easy, customers like it *(and it doesn't cost anything),* but almost no one ever says they're sorry. Then, immediately after you apologize, fix the problem while the customer is still there. *(If you can, or ASAP.)*

- **You want people to hold your feet to the fire.** By setting high standards for yourself, you'll encourage a certain percentage of people to seek out every potential flaw. Good. It gives you another reason to eliminate those flaws.

- **Everybody has a bad day.** Even customers. If they lose their temper, forgive them. Go out of your way to make them feel comfortable about coming back. (They might be a little embarrassed.)

- **The customer is always right—up to a point.** Your job is to figure out what that point is. We stretch pretty far to decide in the customer's favor. You should too. It's profitable.

- **Be taken advantage of with a smile.** If you've decided to give the customer what he or she wants, give in completely and cheerfully. Don't haggle over the amount, and don't roll your eyes or be sarcastic. If you are anything less than cheerful, it will cost you all the good will you were trying to gain.

- **Let the customer help you provide good service.** Teach them how to get the best service; when it's a good time to come see you; and what they need to tell you in order to get the job done right the first time.

- **Explain to customers how you do things.** You may have the world's best system for getting things done, but if your customers don't understand it, they're likely to be confused at best—and angry at worst. Once they understand you have systems–and those systems work–they're bound to think better of you and want to come back.

- **How often should you say thank you?** Every time you get a chance.

- **Decide to be the best.** Set your goal at the highest performance standard possible, knowing that if you expect more you're going to get more.

When You Blow It, Make Amends

In the mid-70s, John Mueller worked as a representative for the 3M Company. John sold film used in the printing process. He says, "We lost the business to Kodak; our product did not perform. I not only removed our film, but I picked up the Kodak film, delivered it, and optimized it to minimize downtime. When our new product worked, we got the business back!" Exceed your customer's expectations.

You Can Never Give Too Much

Marketing genius Jay Abraham says that to lift yourself and your company above the competition:

"You cannot service too much.

You cannot educate enough.

You cannot inform too much.

You cannot offer too much follow-up and follow through too far.

You cannot make ordering too easy.

You cannot make calling or coming into your place of business too desirable."

Though we might debate some of these points if we take them apart, I think you understand the spirit of what he's saying. We must do all these things to gain and keep customers. And it's especially important now that we realize that every customer can lead us to others.

What's the Payoff?

I think this chapter shows you that providing exceptional service to your customers will come back to you manyfold in referrals as well as increased business from them.

The better you serve your customers and prospects, the more powerful and "hotter" their referrals will be, and the easier it will be to convert those referral prospects into satisfied customers.

Tom is a printing salesperson in Baltimore. He did a great job with one of his customers, CNN. His customer contact was so happy that she took him around the office bragging about the job and showing it, and him, to other printing buyers within the organization. She wrote him a great testimonial letter and has given him several external referrals to go along with those internal referrals. Tom knows that delivering legendary service helps you grow your business referrals—the most powerful way to sell.

Use Accelerating Actions and Avoid Decelerating Actions

In his book *Selling at Mach 1* (Motivational Resources, 1994), Steven Sullivan lists actions that will either accelerate or decelerate your image in the eyes of your customers. Which of these can you do? Which should you stop doing?

Accelerating Actions

■ Periodically deliver something to eat, the more creative the better.

■ Call or send flowers, candy, etc. on birthdays, anniversaries, and sickness.

■ Give a free lesson of any kind (golf, tennis, skiing, etc.).

■ Give presents for their children.

■ Send music cassettes of customers' favorite artists.

■ Send a postcard to customers while on vacation.

■ Give gift certificates for dinner, movies, video rentals, etc.

■ Bring in ice cream, Popsicles, or sodas on a hot day.

■ Give lottery tickets.

■ Bring desserts for lunch.

■ Give subscriptions to a weekly sports newspaper or other periodical of interest.

■ Use personal thank-you notes.

■ Order your customers personalized stationary.

■ Contribute articles to their newsletters.

■ Arrange trips to your facilities/plant to educate your customers and show your hospitality.

Decelerating Actions

■ Not returning your customers' phone calls promptly.

■ Making disparaging comments to your customers about your competition.

■ Keeping your customers waiting.

■ Dropping by without an appointment. (Call ahead with some of the accelerators).

■ Not responding immediately to customer requests.

■ Complaining to customers when things don't go your way.

■ Arguing with customers.

■ Not thanking customers on a regular basis.

■ Showing displeasure when you do something for a customer that is not in your best interest.

■ Not communicating regularly with customers about everything that affects the relationship.

■ Not understanding your customers' business.

CHAPTER 7

Turn Problems into Jackpots

In *The Marketing Imagination* (Free Press, 1986), Theodore Levitt says, "One of the surest signs of a bad or declining relationship is the absence of complaints from the customer. The customer is either not being candid or not being contacted. Probably both. Communication is impaired. The absence of candor reflects the decline of trust, the deterioration of the relationship."

Many people who write on customer service like to quote a study conducted by the Technical Assistance Research Programs Institute (based in Washington, DC). This study revealed some interesting information.

- For big-ticket durable goods, 40 percent of unhappy customers won't complain.

- For medium-ticket durable goods, 50 percent of unhappy customers won't complain.

- For big-ticket services, 63 percent of unhappy customers won't complain.

- For small-ticket services, 55 percent of unhappy customers won't complain.

This study also discovered that complainers are more likely to do business with the company that upset them than noncomplainers.

The Strategic Planning Institute (Cambridge, Pennsylvania) conducted a similar study that revealed some more interesting information.

■ The average business never hears from 96 percent of its unhappy customers. At least 90 percent of them will not visit or buy from it again.

■ Of customers who register a complaint, 70 percent will do business with the company again if the complaint is resolved.

■ Of customers who have a complaint, 95 percent will do business again if the problem is resolved *quickly*.

These studies confirm what I've believed for a long time: 1) Many people don't like to complain about the *little* stuff that didn't meet their expectations; and 2) It's important that you encourage your customers to complain.

Get Your Customers to Complain

"Why would I want them to complain?" you might ask. "Complaints are not much fun." You want your customers to complain for at least four reasons:

1. If they don't complain, you won't know and can't help fix the problem.

2. If they're having a problem, then it's quite likely that others are having it as well, and you need to fix the system.

3. Research indicates that if they don't complain, they are likely to quietly go to your competition.

4. They are telling lots of other people about their bad experience.

I issue a challenge to every salesperson or company executive: GET YOUR CUSTOMERS TO COMPLAIN! Sure, complaints can be downright tough sometimes, but complaining customers are valuable to you and your business.

You *must* be willing to "be in the complaint." If you just sense your customer is not happy with something, don't stick your head in the sand and hope it will go away. It will, along with the customer. Be willing to step into the problem and be there for them. Walter Winchell once said, "A true friend is someone who walks in when others walk out." That's true of business friends as well.

You see, a relationship that has successfully resolved a problem is stronger than one that's never had a problem. Don't brag about your customers who are problem free. Brag about the ones with whom you have such a good relationship that they communicate everything to you, so that you can work things out quickly.

Hit the "Jackpot"

My friend Gary Glaser is the sales manager at a company in Baltimore called Bindagraphics. His company serves printers in their post-printing needs. As you might imagine, there are plenty of problems and complaints to be had in his industry. But Gary calls problems "jackpots," because he believes inherent in each problem is the opportunity to increase customer loyalty and increase business.

When customers see how you are there for them during problems, they value the depth of the relationship you are able to offer. And their loyalty, public praise, and referrals increase. Also, quite often when there is a problem, higher-ups from the organization get involved in the solution. This is an opportunity for you to meet other influencers in the organization and can lead to more business from them. Problems and complaints are truly jackpots!

What to Do When Someone Complains

Here are my eight steps for handling a complaining customer:

1. **Say "I'm sorry."** These should be the first words out of your mouth. It costs nothing. It isn't admitting fault. You're just sorry they are feeling inconvenienced. These are the most powerful words you can speak to a complaining customer. Saying "I'm sorry" right from the get-go can even keep them from getting angry.

2. **Don't take it personally and get defensive.** If you do, you're likely to make excuses, challenge their perceptions, and point fingers at others. All of these accomplish nothing and make your customers feel that you don't really want to be there for them. You may do it without even realizing it. Has anyone ever complained to you about something in which you had little or no involvement? Were the first words out of your mouth, "I'm sorry this has happened. Let's see what I can do to help."? Or were they something like, "Well, that's not something I had anything to do with, but I'll check into it for you."? You think you're being helpful, but the first message that comes across to your customer is "I'm protecting myself first."

3. **Don't argue.** Nobody ever won an argument with a customer. Even if you "win" and prove you are right, you lose.

4. **Demonstrate your willingness to be in the problem and work hard to find a solution.** Offer your help in a tone of voice that matches their level of concern. If they are getting angry, let them talk as much as possible. Don't get angry back, and don't go away. Just be there for them.

5. **Establish the facts.** If your customer is angry, be a good listener. This lets him or her blow off steam and helps you establish the facts as best you can. You may need to talk to some of your internal customers to verify the facts. This will help to minimize a cus-

tomer's tendency to exaggerate. It will also help you resist the temptation to admit fault of the company (or someone within the company) until you know all the facts.

6. **Resolve the problem quickly.** Studies indicate that the faster you resolve problems, the less damage is done.

7. **Thank customers for bringing their concern to your attention.** This lets them know that you value their complaints, so they'll let you know the next time something goes wrong.

8. **Follow through and follow up.** Follow through on getting the problem solved as soon as you can. Go to the customer's office and meet face to face if appropriate (it usually is!). Even if you turn the problem over to someone else in your company, never lose track of it. Make sure they receive an acceptable solution. Then follow up a little bit later. Let them know you've been thinking about the situation and want to make sure everything is really OK. Give them permission to complain again; they may have a little more they need to get off their chest.

Remember, *you* are your company's customer service department!

Deliver Bad News Right Away

If something is going wrong with a customer's order in a way that will affect the service you ultimately render, let the customer know quickly. First, they may need to protect their relationships with people who are counting on them. Second, they may be able to help you with adjustments to their schedule.

Don't just go to customers with a plea for more time or other things that you need *them* to do. Before you call them with the potential problem, think through a few alternatives. Let them know that you are not just asking them to make accommodations; you're working hard on your end as well.

Take Their Satisfaction Temperature

Now that you know the value of the complaining customer and that you need to give them opportunities to complain, I suggest you make a habit of taking your customers' *satisfaction temperature* on a regular basis. The nature of your business will determine how often that is for you (annually, semiannually, quarterly, monthly?).

When I was selling printing and electronic prepress services, about every six months I would take my customers' satisfaction temperature. I tried to do it in person. I'd start by saying something like, "Barbara, I have an important question to ask you. It's important for me to be clear on how well we are serving you. On a scale of 1 to 10, with 1 being miserable and 10 being terrific, how are we doing?"

If I got a 7 or below, I knew I had some unexpressed complaints that needed to be dealt with. If I got an 8 or 9, I wanted to see what it would take, in their eyes, for us to do even better.

Another question I've been asking lately is, "What one thing can you think of that could have made this experience better?"

Whenever I ask for a satisfaction temperature, I always get great stuff to help me do a better job with all my customers, and I know my customers appreciate my genuine concern for their "business happiness."

In *Relationship Selling,* Jim Cathcart provides these guidelines for a formal account review.

1. Review their original purpose for becoming a customer. Re-establish what it was that brought that customer to you in the first place.

2. Determine what their experience was when they first started using your product or service. Did they find it helpful? Were there any problems? Were those problems solved?

3. Determine what their experiences were after they had been using your product or service for some time.

4. Review their experience with the service you and your company have been providing. Do they like the service they've been getting? Are they ready to expand? Do they have additional questions?

5. Do a new diagnosis of their needs. Determine what direction they plan to take in the future.

6. Write a new prescription. Determine how you can meet their needs for the future.

As a selling tool, I like to tell prospects, "When you do business with us, you can expect me to schedule a service review every six months. This will ensure that you have every opportunity to give us your honest feedback about how we are serving you and how we can meet your needs for the future."

Whether it's a formal review or an informal one, do it! Do it in person if you can. And do it on a regular basis, with all your customers.

Practice the Sunset Rule

This rule says, "Never let the sun set on a problem without first calling your customer." Obviously, if you've already agreed to a callback time, then you don't have to call at the end of the day. However, in many circumstances, practicing this rule will exceed customers' expectations and just may help them sleep a little easier.

The Chinese word for *crisis* is composed of two picture-characters. One means *danger* and the other means *opportunity*. Every complaint and every problem is a "jackpot." One dictionary defines jackpot as "winning when the stakes are high." Don't miss these opportunities to set yourself apart from your competition. If you want to build your business on referrals and word-of-mouth, jackpots are the most difficult and most powerful place to start.

CHAPTER 8

Lower Stress Means Higher Loyalty

"It is the stress in people's lives and their assumptions about what will make some of that stress go away that determine what and where they buy. The real value that you bring to anyone's life is in making some of their stress go away. To the extent that you understand their stress better than your competitors, make it go away better than your competitors, and effectively communicate that powerful message, you will become their preferred supplier." So says Donald Cooper in his powerful audiotape program, *Human Marketing: How to Become the Preferred Supplier of What You Sell* (The Donald Cooper Corp., 1995).

People experience stress about what you sell. They may experience stress from their current salesperson. Their stress may be caused by not having what you sell. They probably have tension and stress around the selling process. And they may have stress in how you are selling or servicing them now. They have stress when you arrive in their life, stress during the sale, and stress after the sale has been made. It's Cooper's premise, and I agree, that identifying and reducing these stresses will put you head and shoulders above your competition.

To do this, you have to really get to know your prospects and customers. What is life like for them? In the serving spirit of this book, you want to help them even if it has nothing to do with what you sell. Of course, you'd like them to make a purchase from you if it's appropriate. However, any way you can help them reduce their stress will go a long way toward building trust and making the sale.

Learn to Sense Stress

As you sell and serve your customers, you must become a master at sensing their level of stress and responding appropriately. If they are stressed, you don't want to respond to them in a laid-back manner. Show that you understand the importance of their situation. Cooper tells of a letter he needed to send as part of a proposal for a contract worth $60,000. The woman who typed his letters charged $6 per letter. To him it was a $60,000 letter. To her it was a $6 letter. Unfortunately, she didn't respond to this task with his sense of urgency. She gave him a $6 response to his $60,000 need. He was left feeling frustrated and dissatisfied. Instead of working to relieve some of his stress, she contributed to it.

> "You must understand fully the value and importance of what you do from the customer's point of stress."
>
> Donald Cooper

Some customers will communicate their stresses to us quite clearly. But many will not. We must have our antenna tuned to picking it up. We must ask good questions that help us detect their areas of stress as they relate to what we sell and how we serve them. People who are indirect in their communication style may hold back in letting us know how important something is to them. We need to detect their true need and respond more powerfully.

Cooper says, "You must understand fully the value and importance of what you do from the customer's point of stress." When your customer calls, there is probably some stress-related reason. If she has to leave a message, she is left with that stress until she hears from you. Always return customers' calls right away; get a beeper and cellular phone, and give them your home phone number. Have your voice-mail message state when you'll be back in the office and whom they can contact in an emergency.

Think and Feel Like Your Customers

In this section of the book, we're talking about exceeding customer expectations. When Donald Cooper was the owner of an extremely successful women's clothing store, he became a master at exceeding his customers' expectations. He didn't use traditional research to determine what they expected; he thought and felt like a customer. Then he used his creativity and imagination to implement his strategies.

His customers (and especially their spouses) expected a place to sit down for a few minutes. So Cooper used his creativity and exceeded that expectation by providing electric reclining massage chairs. He says, "I wanted something so that when they came to my store they'd sit down and go 'Wow.' And they'd laugh and have fun. They'd tell others about it." I can only imagine the response of the men who came in with their women. They probably sat back, got a little sleepy, and said, "Take all the time you need, honey. I'm fine."

The Four Currencies

There are four currencies in people's lives: Money, Time, Feeling Safe, and Feeling Special. "Most people think there is only one currency, therefore, they can think of only one way to compete. But when you realize that there are four currencies in people's lives, there are hundreds of ways to compete," states Cooper. He suggests you make a list of how you can exploit the currencies other than money. What can *you* do to save your customers time, help them feel safe, or give them a special experience every time you serve them?

As customers, you and I often receive inferior service because of the transgressions of others. Signs in clothing stores limit us to three items in the changing room; other signs tell us not to bring food or beverages into the store; and we aren't allowed to use the telephone if our shopping spree is making us late for another commitment. In his store, Alive & Well, Cooper broke all the rules. He invited shoppers to take as many items into the changing rooms as they wished. Result: they bought more merchandise. He provided a free beverage bar. Result: people stayed in the store longer. He provided four courtesy phones so people could make local calls. Result: people shopped longer and bought more. His customer washrooms included changing tables with three sizes of diapers, diaper wipes, and cream. Result: mothers of young children were amazed and told all of their friends. And since their *experience* of Alive & Well was always a pleasant one, they came back again and again.

I think seeing your customers from the point of view of their stress can be a very powerful way to examine how you sell and serve your customers. I want to acknowledge Donald Cooper's unique perspective.

Six Steps to Reduce Stress

In his tape program, Cooper shares his six steps to the creative process to reduce customer stress:

1. Using your new and improved understanding of your customers' stress, make a complete list of those stresses in three categories: stress about life in general, buying what you sell, and specifically buying from you.

2. Define your business by how you add value to people's lives, and list the specific ways you will add that value better than your competitors. This will become your service mission.

3. Discipline yourself to look at your business through your customers' eyes—inside and out. Study every part of your business to make sure that you are noticed, remembered, trusted, and preferred.

4. Open your mind and heart to new possibilities. Challenge your assumptions and the assumptions of those around you. Create an environment of intellectual integrity and curiosity.

5. Learn how to use everyday events to jump-start your own creativity . . . every day.

6. Know when you need help in the creative process and carefully hire the best people you can afford. You are the manager of the creative process, but that doesn't mean you have to do it all yourself.

The Second Cornerstone

Form Referral Alliances

Other People Will Help You Succeed

One key to building your business from referrals is forming relationships of mutual support, in which each person helps the other build his or her respective businesses. It's based on the concept that the more you give, the more you get. I call these relationships *referral alliances.*

I've identified three types of referral alliances. First are satisfied customers who, long after you've served them, keep giving you referrals, advice, and other connections. Second are individuals who may never become customers of yours but who are in a position to give you referrals. Then there are referral allies who may never be in a position to give you direct referrals but who can help you advance your sales with their advice, wisdom, coaching, and contacts. This section will help you meet and build relationships with all three types of referral alliances.

Is Networking Dead?

Networking is an overused word and an underused strategy among many salespeople. Networking has been around as long as humans have been on this earth. It's definitely not dead. These days, when many people think of networking, they think of going to business events or specific networking events. But networking is so much more than an event. It's a way of doing business and a way to generate substantial referrals.

Bob Burg, author of *Endless Referrals: Network Your Everyday Contacts into Sales* (McGraw-Hill, 1994), says, "Real networking is the cultivation of mutually beneficial, give and take, win/win relationships." When done correctly and with genuine care for the success of others in your network, this results in an enormous increase in referrals.

Harvey Mackay published a little book called *The Rolodex Network Builder* (Mackay Envelope Corp., 1993). In it he says, "If I had to name the single characteristic shared by all the truly successful people I've met in my lifetime, I'd have to say it's the ability to create and nurture a network of contacts."

I use the term *referral alliances* instead of networking because I want to emphasize two important points: a strategy (your network of contacts becomes well thought out, part of your overall selling strategy) and an alliance (your network of contacts is not just a bunch of people you know). You have nurtured relationships with everyone (to one degree or another). You work together to bring each other as many win/win opportunities as possible.

Since my referral alliances concept and networking are close kin, I'd like to share a couple of definitions of networking from some notable authorities on the topic, whom I will quote heavily throughout this section of the book.

Lynne Waymon is one of this country's leading experts on networking. Lynne says, "Networking, in its pure form, enables business people to further their own goals while helping others further theirs. It should be a positive step in the right direction for everyone on the road to success. Networking is a process of building business relationships for the long term."

Bob Burg says networking is "the building, cultivating, and developing of a very large and diverse group of people who will gladly and continually refer you lots and lots of business, while you, in turn, do the same for them." He also says, "All things being equal, people will do business with and refer business to those people who they know, like, and trust."

Dr. Ivan Misner, in *The World's Best Known Marketing Secret*, writes, "Networks are coalitions of business professionals who, through a mutual support system, help each other do more business . . . it must be based on the concept that *givers gain*." The mutual support system that he mentions can come from a specific organization that assists people in networking, from networking events, or from other external sources. Or it can come from what you build with your own initiative and creativity. The point is, you must begin to ally yourself with people who can help you obtain more referrals.

Contact Spheres

Dr. Misner writes about a concept similar to my referral alliances, but he calls it *contact spheres*. "This is a group of businesses or professionals that can provide you with a steady source of leads," he writes. "They tend to work in areas that complement rather than compete with your business. For example, if you were to put a lawyer, a CPA, a financial planner, and a banker in the same room for an hour, you couldn't stop them from doing business. Each of them has clients or customers that could benefit from services of the others."

Every salesperson needs leads for new business. I'm suggesting that you go one step further, and make sure your referral alliances give you not just leads, but warm referrals.

Misner shares some examples of contact spheres:

1. Graphic communication businesses: Printers, graphic artists, specialty advertising agents, marketing consultants. (*I'll add: paper salespeople, color separators, and noncompeting printers and artists.*)

2. Real-estate services: Residential agents, commercial agents, escrow companies, title companies, mortgage brokers. *(Mark Sheer would add: photographers, contractors, plumbers, caterers, gardeners, exterminators, home inspectors, florists, and roofers. I'll add: Realtors® in other towns.)*

3. Contractors: Painters, carpenters, plumbers, landscapers, electricians. *(I'll add: roofers, floor companies, and fence companies.)*

4. Business equipment vendors: In telecommunications, computers, photocopiers.

5. Special-occasion services: Photographers, caterers, travel agents, florists. *(I'll add: musicians, DJs, bakers, event planners, tent companies.)*

Kevin Kelley is a sales manager for Metro Graphic Communications. One of its products is business forms. Kevin has formed referral alliances with other commercial printers. When his printer alliances run across a customer or prospect who needs forms, they always refer Kevin. Even though Kevin's company can do some of the other types of printing, these referral alliances trust him not to go after their commercial business.

Have I touched on any area of yours? If not, think of other types of businesses that complement yours. How can you begin to ally yourself with others?

I was giving a presentation in Greensboro, North Carolina. I had arranged with an airport transportation service to be driven from the hotel to the airport for my flight home. Arthur Goodman picked me up and we got to talking. Arthur owns a business he calls Designated Driver. He and his drivers are on call to assist people who have had too much to drink and need a ride home. What is unique about Arthur's business is that he not only drives the customer home but drives the customer's car home as well.

Arthur's business is booming because of his ability to form referral alliances. He has made alliances with bartenders, the ABC board, restaurants, police officers, and others. Each of these groups of alliances serves Arthur with referrals, and Arthur serves them too, by making their jobs easier. This can work for everyone who has something to sell.

You May Already Be Using Referral Alliances

You may have already formed some referral alliances. If so, you already know how they can help you gather referrals that turn into sales. The key questions are: Are you doing it as effectively as you could be? Are you constantly looking for new alliances? Are you investing the time to nurture and deepen the relationships you form, so that each party knows exactly what the other does and how they benefit their respective customers?

Misner says, "To get the most out of Contact Spheres, 1) identify as many professions as possible that fit within your own Contact Sphere; 2) identify specific individuals who could fit into your Contact Sphere by going to various networking organizations, consulting your Rolodex or card files, and reconsider the professionals you may presently be referring; and 3) invite each party to participate in networking groups with you so you can formalize your relationship."

Beyond Networking

Dr. Misner is big on networking organizations and their corresponding events. In fact, he's the founder of Business Network International (headquartered in Claremont, California). His company helps people all over the world organize themselves into what he calls "strong-contact networks." These groups meet weekly to exchange leads and referrals. They restrict membership to only one person per profession or specialty and structure their meeting formats to make sure referral exchanges are taking place. For some industries and professions, these formal networking groups can be extremely helpful. If you want to learn how to get the most out of such groups, I highly recommend his book and his organization (Business Network International at 909-624-2227 inside Southern California and 800-825-8286 elsewhere).

What I'm talking about goes beyond these networking organizations and networking events. To build a business in which you work only from referrals, you need to tune your awareness to everyone who comes into your life who might become a referral alliance. Stop and think about the types of people you should be meeting and with whom you should be nurturing referral relationships. Be open to people who at first glance may not look like good prospects, but might become great allies. When your awareness is tuned into forming these types of relationships, more opportunities will present themselves.

> **A referral from another salesperson can be as powerful as a referral from a satisfied customer.**

For me, a writer and professional speaker, other speakers can be powerful allies. A little later I'll tell you how I obtained a significant number of speaking engagements as the direct result of serving another speaker.

A referral from another salesperson can be as powerful as a referral from a satisfied customer. Let's say, for example, your salesperson ally is in the office of one of his customers, and that customer needs something the salesperson can't deliver. If that salesperson knows how you benefit your customers, he can recommend you with confidence and enthusiasm. He will be a hero to the customer, and you have a hot referral to pursue. All the goodwill and trust he has established with his customer gets transferred to you. In this scenario, you'd have to really blow it not to make the sale.

I know several printing salespeople who have allied themselves with salespeople from other printing companies with whom there is little or no competition. They each get so many referred leads that they don't have to make cold calls anymore.

Dr. Misner says, "The only people who are going to make referrals for you consistently are people who know you and trust you: your friends, associates, customers, clients, peers, and family members. [I would add referral alliances.] You need to start spending time with the right people in structured professional environments."

Bird-Dogging

Joe Girard uses a technique he calls "hunting with bird dogs." Basically, he pays his customers and referral alliances a small reward for anyone they send him who makes a purchase. He's unabashed about asking people to help him build his business, and he pays the "finder's fee" without hesitation. This technique may or may not be appropriate for you and your business, but it's a concept worth considering.

Marilyn Jennings, the most successful real estate agent in Canada, tells her customers that she doesn't pay for leads. "After all," she writes, "they wouldn't feel very good about their friend having referred them to me, if they knew he was getting paid for doing so."

So what can you do if paying referral alliances cash isn't appropriate for you and your business? Girard suggests a gift certificate to a nice restaurant or something similar. This way you are still rewarding them, but it's not so blatant as cash. In fact, you can form an alliance relationship with a couple of nice restaurants. If they sell you gift certificates at a discount, you'll bring them a steady stream of business—much of it new business to them. If the restaurant does its job well, those new folks will return.

Girard goes on to say, "One of my favorite sources of bird dogs is barbers. They do a lot of talking to their customers. I try to get a haircut at a different barbershop in my area every time I need one. Thus, I can circulate among a lot of barbers and recruit them and bolster their interest."

This technique illustrates the creativity you can use in building your alliances for referrals.

The Win/Win Alliance

Your alliances should be productive for everyone involved. There are some important things you must do to make sure your referral alliances become a productive source of referrals for you. First, you must find ways to serve them.

1. Give them referrals.

2. Help them solve needs or problems through your network of contacts.

3. Give them advice.

4. Be a good listener when they need one.

5. Find out what success means to them, and help them when you can.

Second, you want to make sure that they know exactly what you do and how you benefit your customers or clients. Meet occasionally to remind and update each other. Tell each other specific stories about how you've served your customers. Tell them how you've solved customers' problems or really come to the rescue for them. The more your referral alliances know about how you've saved others time or money, or made others more money, the more excited they can be when they refer you to a new prospect. Get your referral alliances excited about what you do, so they can transfer that enthusiasm to others when the opportunity presents itself. Get excited about what they do as well. Now you have a bunch of quality people bragging about each other to prospects.

Third, you must work your network. Misner says, "It's not called net-sit, or net-eat, it's called Net-Work, and if you want to build a prosperous word-of-mouth-based business, you must work. Find ways to stay in touch with your allies. Merely by knowing them is not enough; you must nurture the relationships."

> "Lofty words cannot construct an alliance or maintain it; only concrete deeds do that."
>
> John F. Kennedy

Your referral alliances must have a clear handle on who a good prospect is for you, on how you truly serve your customers, and on the types of people you like to add to your network. Put them on your mailing list to receive all your promotional literature, newsletters, and the like. Whenever you run across an article on a subject that you know some of them will appreciate, mail it out. I'm working on a weekly newsletter that I intend to fax not only to my clients and prospective clients, but also to my allies. Since the fax will contain valuable information that they can use, I will be serving them as I remind them.

Tom Winninger, in his book *Price Wars* (St. Thomas Press, 1994), writes, "If you are going to be the best at what you do, surround yourself with [people] who are the best at what they do. Make sure that your [alliance] is made up of people who have the same value merchant philosophy you have."

Turn Salespeople into Your Allies

I'd like to share with you a story of how I turned another salesperson into a referral ally. I had written an article for Printing Industries of America that was published nationwide. A salesperson by the name of Tom saw it and called to see if I had any more articles or other information that could help him sell more printing. We chatted for a few minutes, and I began to slowly create a referral alliance relationship with him (for my sales workshops).

I asked him a few qualifying questions, and his company fit the profile. I asked whom I should contact and tried to warm up the referral to his boss. After a few minutes, I could tell he was growing reluctant to go much further, so I told him I'd send him some things right away and ended the conversation.

A week or so later, I called to make sure he had received my packet. I then proceeded to warm up the referral a bit more. This time he was much more receptive. Why? Because he had already tried one of my techniques and it had resulted in some new business. He was beginning to like me and trust me a little more. And I had now served him even better.

I asked him to send me some information on his company, and he agreed. I also asked if he would be willing to hand-deliver my information to his boss, and he agreed to that as well.

The information packet he sent me included a note asking for my critique of the package. Aha—another opportunity to serve this referral alliance. (Don't get me wrong. Tom was more than just a potential referral. I like him, and I want to do whatever I can to help him grow his business.)

The story isn't over. My next step is to send Tom my information and have him hand-deliver it to my prospect, the owner of the company. Once they've had a chance to talk about me and about Tom's increasing success, I will call the owner.

Forming an alliance turned what could have been just a very brief encounter with a salesperson into a pretty strong referral. This salesperson had already used one of my techniques to bring in more business for himself and the company. Tom told me that the other salespeople had read my article and were lobbying to bring me in for some workshops. Could I ask for a better introduction to a new prospect?

A Foolproof Referral Strategy

Your referral alliances will give you referrals because:

1. You've served them well and they want to pay you back.
2. They want to be heroes to one of their customers, clients, or associates.
3. They know that helping you will come back to them, one way or another.
4. They truly want to contribute to your success, because they like you and trust you.

I know some salespeople who have built incredible careers using this referral alliance strategy. Just as referral selling is more than a bunch of techniques (it is a way of thinking), so too is this concept of forming referral alliances. You move through life acting on the knowledge that building strong, mutually beneficial relationships with people, even those who may never buy what you sell, will take you to higher levels of success.

Have a Business Event Strategy

S ince going to business events is a significant part of forming referral alliances, I wanted to provide you with some solid information on the subject. To that end, I decided to interview a nationally known expert in the art and skill of networking and building business contacts, Lynne Waymon. Lynne is the co-author (with Anne Baber) of two popular books on networking, *Great Connections: Small Talk and Networking for Business People* (Impact Publications, 1992) and *52 Ways to Reconnect, Follow Up, and Stay in Touch, When You Don't Have Time to Network* (Kendall/Hunt Publishing, 1994).

My interview with Lynne will introduce different aspects of effective networking at business events. This interview will run throughout the entire section.

I will supplement her ideas with some of my own, as well as those of other experts in the field.

BC: Lynne, networking is such a business buzzword. What is good business networking?

LW: Bill, I found the answer to this question in the most amazing place! I saw a show on the Disney Channel the other night that said it all. The show was about a tribe in New Guinea that bestows leadership not on the person who has accumulated the most, but on the person who has given the most away. That's what networking is about—attracting people by giving. Giving resources, information, attention, support, referrals. Of course there are things you'd like to find or learn or connect with, but do the giving and the getting will take care of itself.

BC: To use networking effectively, does it help to have a networking strategy?

LW: Well, don't be like the guy who said to me, "I tried networking last Thursday. It doesn't work!" The best strategy is to think long-term. Networking is exchanging information, resources, and ideas in such a way that it builds the relationship. It's not just meeting a potential customer; it's building a long-term, mutually beneficial relationship.

Another part of strategy is to have a good networking mindset. I'm amazed how many of us approach groups of people with thoughts like "I hate this small talk. I ought to be back at the office. I can't think of anything to say." In my workshops, I say good networking means mind over mouth. As you go to a meeting, whether it's a backyard barbecue or a networking luncheon, program your mind to say to you, "I wonder who I'm going to meet here." "I'm going to really learn five people's names." "I have lots of topics I'd like to explore with people here."

So, think long-term, think mind over mouth. And think about your six-million-person network. Yes, you can have access to six million people. Here's how it works. Do you think you know 50 people, Bill? Neighbors, relatives, past co-workers, teachers? If each of those 50 people knows 50 people, you now know 2,500 people who are friends of friends. If each of them knows 50 people, you now know 125,000 people. If each of them knows 50 people, you now have access to six million people who are only three or four people away from you—if you know what to ask for.

At a business event or networking meeting, here's the range of people with whom you want to connect:

1. Actual prospects.

2. People who work for companies that you'd like to prospect.

3. Candidates for your referral alliance who can generate referrals for you.

4. Candidates for your referral alliance who can help you with advice, wisdom, and their network.

5. Interesting people representing interesting products and services who become part of your personal catalog of products and services. You can use these to help yourself and others at some later date.

BC: In your book, you mention four stages of networking. What are they?

LW: The first one is all too common, yet it's one to avoid. It's called Taking. The "Me, me, me" attitude. It's saying, "Hi. I sell specialty advertising products. If you ever need anything, give me a call. Bye now." Like kissing too soon on the first date, it's offensive and rarely leads to good relationships.

The second stage is called Trading—a little more productive. That's when I own a tree-cutting service and you need to have trees cut down. But you can have so much more, which leads to the third stage, Teaching. See networking as a process of teaching people about you and your business—and, of course, learning about them and their business.

The fourth and highest stage of networking is Trusting. The best networkers build trust by showing, over the long haul, their character and competence. Where trust has been built, referrals will flow freely.

BC: Part of good networking is joining certain key organizations. How do you choose the right organizations?

LW: Choose some groups because of the resources, referrals, and support you can get. Choose others because your clients are there.

Choose organizations that have a good networking culture. When you go to the meetings, do people seem upbeat, interested, interesting? Are there ways for people to meet each other? Are newcomers welcomed and are there ways to become visible? Is the organization growing and thriving or dying and depressing?

BC: What do I do to make it worth my time?

LW: Joining is not enough. You can pay your dues and read the newsletter and attend events—and still not have a network. You have to get visible to make it worth the time. Contribute your skills, give out name tags, make an announcement, write a newsletter article. By the way, introduce yourself to the speaker and officers. Tell them what you're interested in. You may even get mentioned by the speaker. That's visibility.

Rick Hill, a professional speaker and author, suggests that you don't join an organization just to get leads. Join because you want to get involved. If you're there just for leads, you'll probably come on too strong or give up too early (not to mention always be in a "taking" mode). Rick says that if you enjoy the work the association does, then you'll get involved, and better-quality leads will result. These will be stronger referrals and much easier to come by.

I can't emphasize this point enough. If you are going to take the time and expense to join an association, the best way to get referrals from it is to become active in it. When I was first getting started as a professional speaker, I made a great decision (in all humility). I joined the National Speakers Association and the Washington, DC, local chapter, the National Capital Speakers Association.

I was there to hang out and learn from people who did what I did. I knew it would help me build my business, but I never thought I'd get business directly from the association.

In my second year of membership, our local chapter was led by a hard-working professional named Wolf Rinke. (If you ever need a great speaker, just cry Wolf.) Anyway, during Wolf's tenure as president of our chapter, I worked hard on our first speaker's school.

A month or so after the school took place, Wolf gave me a call. He had been contacted by a company in Atlanta, Sommers Communications, which had just won a large seminar contract and needed several high-quality speakers. It was not the right match for Wolf, so he wondered if I was interested. He told me that one reason he called me was that I had worked hard for him. (I served him!)

Well, my contract with Sommers Communications has resulted in a long-term relationship: well over 150 paid speaking engagements to date. That's significant!

Don't expect to get business from an organization unless you truly get involved, get visible, and serve others.

BC: All of us have limited time to spend in the networking phase of business development. How do we decide what will yield the best results?

LW: Think of a bull's-eye with concentric circles. On the outside rim are Acquaintances, on the next inner ring are the Associates, then come the Actors, then the Advocates, and finally the Allies.

Acquaintances: There's no circle around these folks, because they barely know who you are. You bump into them from time to time. You're not in their network and they're not in yours. An acquaintance is usually a nonproductive relationship. To create productivity with these people, you must upgrade them to associates.

Associates: You see these people regularly because you have chosen to join a group that brings you into contact with them, or both of you are pursuing contact with each other outside of any formal group. Since you are meeting regularly, you have the opportunity to get to know each other in your respective areas of competence. As you begin to know and appreciate each other, opportunities for referrals and other help begin to grow. Mutually beneficial exchanges will flourish as you and your contacts become associates.

Actors: Think of actors on a stage. They are in a dialogue. Something's happening between them. Actors are the people in your life with whom you are actively exchanging valuable information and resources. Over time, as trust grows, you become interested in adding to each other's success. When you really tune into what your contact is looking for, you move him or her from an associate to an actor.

Advocates: Advocates are people who go out of their way to find opportunities to refer and recommend you to others. They are so confident in your abilities and your integrity that they are willing to put their good names on the line to promote you. Advocates make sure the people you want to meet hear about you before they hear from you.

Allies: Think of these people as being your very own board of trustees. They care about your success. They give you advice that you respect because they have become experts on you. They cheer you on in every arena of your life. They give you a nudge when you most need it. They celebrate your successes with as much enthusiasm as you do theirs. You won't have time to cultivate too many relationships at this intense level, so you must select these people carefully.

One word of warning: You'll be labeled a "nuisance networker" if you violate the natural progression of networking contacts. You must allow the trust to develop comfortably for all parties.

Notice where you are with people. If you want to have a more active relationship with someone in your circle of contacts, you can always make the next move.

CHAPTER 11

Make a
Great Connection

BC: I have a meeting coming up where I'm going to be in a room full of other businesspeople. Should I plan ahead or just let things happen spontaneously?

LW: Wouldn't it be great if great connections always happened spontaneously? Unfortunately, what often happens is a conversation like this:
Hi, how are you?
I'm fine. How about you?
Just great. What's new?
Not much. Busy. What are you up to?
Oh, same old grind.

That's a conversation in search of a topic.

So instead, be *prepared* to be spontaneous. Plan your answer to the question "How are you?" or "What's new?" Tell about a resource you've found, a client you helped, some "win" you've just had—and tell it with enthusiasm! And be ready to ask about things you'd like to find, or learn, or connect with. When someone says, "What's new?," have your agenda ready.

I like to come to events ready to talk about one major win I've just had and one challenge I'm facing. I get out of the "What's new?" dead end by saying, "Let me tell you about a great win I just had, and then you can tell me one." Usually a good conversation will develop. Sometimes people thank me for helping them remember the good stuff that's happening in their lives.

BC: What about having goals for the event?

LW: That's a great idea. Examples might be, "I'm going to meet five new people tonight," or "I'm going to reconnect with Fred," or "I'm going to ask Susan to introduce me to the program chair."

Lynne is right. I used to be terrible at business events at which I didn't know very many people. So, I've turned to goals to help me get better. For example:

1. Have significant conversations with at least three new people.

2. Meet the speaker and have a good conversation. See if I can serve her.

3. Have a conversation with the association leader. Serve her in some way.

4. Introduce at least two people to each other.

Setting little goals like these usually keeps me from wimping out. The only thing that commits me to the goals is my word to myself. Do I ever slip? Of course. When I keep my word, do I get good stuff? You bet!

BC: I'm generally not a shy person, but at business events I become shy. How can I learn how to get conversations started?

LW: Be prepared with a few openers such as, "What brings you to tonight's meeting?" or "This is my first time here. Have you been a member long?" or "I came here hoping to meet other people who have home-based businesses. Is that why you're here?"

One more tip. Make sure your body language reflects your desire to meet people. All too often I see people standing around with a vaguely bored look on their faces, eating another olive. Instead, smile, look confident and go out of your way to greet people. Just last night I made a wonderful contact by introducing myself to someone in the hotel lobby who was obviously looking for the same meeting I was.

Bob Burg says, "When meeting a networking prospect for the first time, invest 99.9 percent of the conversation in asking questions about that person and their business. They want to talk about their business, not yours—let them. The people who we find most interesting are the people who seem most interested in us."

Jeffrey Gitomer, author of *The Sales Bible* (Morrow, 1994) says, "Early in the event, stand by the entrance if possible. This way you can see everyone and establish your targets."

Sometimes I'll offer to assist with registration for a while. This sets me up as a host. I can see who's coming in and meet them, and then it's easier to approach them later.

Gitomer also says, "Spend 75 percent of your time with people you don't know. Hanging around with fellow employees and old friends is fun but won't help you meet other important people. Spend 25 percent of your time building existing relationships." Find new ways to serve them and tell them stories of how you've served others.

BC: What about when everyone else seems to know each other? How do I join one of those clumps of people already engaged in conversation?

LW: Well, one of the best networkers I know tells me she never joins clumps. She just goes up to someone who's standing alone and makes her own clump. But if you do join a group, be ready with "May I join you?" Or say, "How do you all know each other?" if they pause. More likely, the person who's talking will continue, so that's your cue to pace them. If they're smiling, you smile. If they're looking serious, you look serious. Indicate with your body language that you want to participate, not interrupt.

BC: I'm absolutely awful at remembering names. Any tips for me?

LW: It's not surprising that so many people say, "I never can remember names." The next time you're at an event, count the number of seconds people spend in the name exchange. What's your guess, Bill?

BC: Ten seconds?

LW: No, about five seconds! The key here is to linger longer over the names. Ask about the other person's name. "Is that Linda with a *y* or an *i?*" "Do you like to be called William or Bill?" And be ready to teach them your name. Nothing fancy here, just a tip for remembering. I often say, "My name's Lynne with an *e*. And years later that person will say "Hi, Lynne with an *e*." Speak slowly and give your first name twice. Say, "Hi, I'm Bill, Bill Cates."

I've started helping people remember my name by saying, "Hi, I'm Bill Cates. That's Cates with a *C*, not Bill Gates, with a *G*." Then we usually have a conversation about how it's too bad I'm not Bill Gates, the founder and CEO of Microsoft (whose net worth is about $13 billion). We get a little laugh at my expense, and guess what? They remember my name.

BC: I know that a lot of people seem to struggle when asked, "What do you do?" What should I say?

LW: Avoid your job title, avoid jargon, avoid an industry label, such as "I'm in sales." Tell your talent, not your title. Plan ahead to tell in two sentences one of your talents and a recent example of a project, success, or completion. Instead of "I'm a professional speaker," or "I'm a networking expert," I might say, "I get people talking to each other at conventions. Last week I did a workshop for 300 people at the National Association of Home Builders convention." If you do this, it will be easy for people to get into conversation with you—and you'll be giving them a vivid picture of your competence and character.

Bob Burg recommends that you have an opening statement prepared that says what you do and how it benefits others.

"When someone asks what you do, don't just say, 'I'm in advertising.' Or 'I sell insurance.' Or 'I sell printing.' A better statement would be, 'I help people create long-term wealth and immediate security through insurance.' Or 'I am a printing consultant. I help people get the best possible printed piece at a competitive price.'"

You get the idea. You can say what you do, and then follow it with a simple benefit statement.

I suggest you talk about your job in a way that makes you look different from all the other people who do what you do. Tell them what makes you different. This will help you stand out from the crowd in their minds. It will help them remember you. And it might trigger an interesting conversation.

Let me share how I've tried to differentiate myself from the thousands of people who write and talk on the subject of sales. Sales speakers are a dime a dozen. Good sales speakers are a quarter a dozen. It didn't take me long to learn that I had to find a way to separate myself from the crowd. So I decided to become this country's foremost expert in how to build a business on referrals. Although I do write and speak on other aspects of the sales process, I always lead with this distinguishing feature. There are only a handful of people who have this "referral" focus. This focus helps people see how I'm different from other sales experts.

BC: What are good topics for me to bring up? What topics are more likely to lead to business exchanges?

LW: Any topic that you have enthusiasm and energy for. It could be a personal interest such as coaching a kid's soccer team, or it might be a business project, such as learning to use a new kind of software on your computer.

And listen for topics they're interested in. Listen generously, with an ear for how the resources and information you have might help them succeed in business and with personal interests, too.

Conversation Starters

Always be looking for ways to serve these people you meet. They may become referral alliances. The better you serve them, the more likely they will serve you if and when they can. Go to these events ready to give, and you'll truly stand out (and will receive).

To establish rapport and to learn ways to serve, ask good questions and be a good listener. Most people like talking about themselves and their businesses. Just as you use good questions to probe your prospects, do the same with people you meet at business events. Get them talking. Learn about their challenges as well as their successes. Be a focused, active listener. Who might become prospects or referral alliances? Gain their trust and then serve them. (Even if they aren't candidates for future business, you can still serve them. It's fun to do—and you never know how it might come back to help you.)

Bob Burg offers these questions to ask at networking and other business events:

1. How did you get started in the widget business?

2. What do you enjoy most about your profession?

3. What separates your company from your competition? (This will allow them to brag, or it will serve them by getting them to think about this important

question. By the way, make sure you have an up-to-date answer.)

4. What advice would you give someone just starting in your industry?

5. What one thing would you do with your business if you knew you could not fail?

6. What significant changes have you seen take place in your profession over the years?

7. What do you see as the coming trend in your business/industry?

8. Describe the strangest or funniest experience you've had in your business.

9. What have you found to be the best ways to promote your business?

10. What one sentence would you like people to use in describing the way you do business?

I like to say, "If I were to introduce you to someone I know you'd like to meet, what one sentence should I use to describe you and the way you do business?"

Here's another one I picked up somewhere. "What do I need to know about you and your business so that when I'm talking to someone, I will know if you should meet her?" Now you are in a position to serve them right there at the meeting. Very powerful!

These are suggestions to get a conversation going. Don't use them all at once. Use them to get things going, and then use your savvy to explore the answers.

When you talk about yourself and your business, make sure you are talking in terms of *benefits*. I know I'm translating my features and advantages into benefits when I'm using phrases like, "which means to you." If you're talking to prospects, show how you can benefit them. If you're talking to possible referral alliances, show them how you benefit your customers.

Tips for Connecting

Don't fire-hose

Sometimes you meet a bona fide prospect at a networking event or other business event—someone with a clear need for what you sell. Don't do what speaker and author Rick Hill calls fire-hosing. Don't do an information dump on them.

Unless you have established some rapport, this behavior will work against you. Ask some questions and explore the prospect's situation. Then, at some point, get his or her card and get permission to have you follow up. You might go for an appointment right then if the rapport is high, or you could wait until a little later in the event.

Whenever I am getting permission to call someone later, I ask, "When I call, will I get straight to you or am I likely to get your voice mail?" Or, jokingly, "Do you have a well-trained gatekeeper?" Sometimes, if I haven't qualified people enough to want an appointment, or if I don't have my calendar with me, I'll schedule a phone appointment for the next day. This way they are expecting my call and I will get past any barriers.

Be an unselfish listener

You must be in a place in your heart and mind where you truly want people to tell their story and you don't care if you tell your story. You're there to meet people and learn about them so you can serve them, so that they will serve you. You must get it through your head that you are not there to tell your story first.

Maintain good eye contact

At business events, good eye contact is important and takes a little more discipline. It's easy to become distracted by friends or colleagues walking by. When you're talking to a new acquaintance and your eyes are wandering, he or she may get the impression that you're just killing time until someone better comes along.

Manage interruptions

Be careful how you allow interruptions by people who know you well. Be gracious and introduce your old friend to your new acquaintance. If you and your acquaintance are getting into a good conversation, you might say to your friend, "Brian, it's great to see you. I was just learning about Terrie's business. Tell you what, give me a few minutes with her, and I'll catch up to you. OK?"

Find a networking buddy

If meeting people at business events is not always easy for you, find someone to go to the event with you. But don't use that person as a crutch for your fear. Rather, make an agreement to introduce people to each other and invite each other into conversations. Introduce each other in glowing terms. Help the whole group get excited about meeting the two of you.

Meet the speaker

If the business event you're attending has a guest speaker, meet the speaker and have a conversation. Make sure he or she knows what you do and how you benefit others. Then sit up front, with your name tag where it is highly visible, and there's a good chance you'll get mentioned in the program. Do this at every meeting and you'll be known by everyone in no time.

The bottom line

Dr. Wolf Rinke, author of *Make It a Winning Life* (Achievement Publishers, 1992), says, "Make sure they walk away feeling glad they've talked to you."

BC: Sometimes I meet people who are super free with how they give out their business cards. I don't know if they are doing it because they think I might be a prospect for them or if they are just trying to create name recognition. Talk to me about the role of business cards at business events.

LW: Don't play bumper cards with your business cards. That's a cardboard connection. Instead, pour your energy into the conversation and look for a reason to exchange cards—a reason to extend the event beyond the event. A reason to call them next Tuesday, or to fax them in two weeks. Wouldn't you rather get back to the office with the cards of five people you know a little better than with the cards of 20 people who wouldn't remember you if they saw you next week?

I always get a kick out of a technique used by Joe Girard (*How to Sell Anything to Anybody*). Joe says that at football games, when everyone was on their feet hollering and waving, he'd reach into a paper bag and throw a handful of his business cards into the air. Later in this book, I will teach you a technique of "seed planting" that will land you tons of referrals from customers and even prospects. I guess Joe saw these business cards as seeds he was sowing in hopes that one or more would take root. Business cards are relatively cheap, so if you sell something that most people are prospects for (Joe sold cars), why not have a little extra fun at your next sporting event?

When you give a business card to a definite referral alliance, say something like, "Here, put this in your wallet so it will be handy when you meet someone who can benefit from my services."

I taught this technique to a mortgage banker, and after the seminar he gave me a card to put in my wallet—which I did. Less than a week later I was in a meeting with a colleague who mentioned he was looking to invest in some real estate. I gave him this guy's card, and they worked together to purchase five investment properties. If that mortgage banker had not been proactive, I wouldn't have been able to help either of them. Needless to say, I was a "hero" to both parties.

BC: If you have a good conversation with a person, what are appropriate ways to reconnect later at that same event?

LW: How about bringing someone over and introducing them? Look for common interests, and be a great connector. You can use any reason: "You both have twins," "You both grew up in Chicago," "You both work in telecommunications."

Before you leave the event, do say good-bye to the two or three people you most want to become known to. Reconfirm when you'll call, or just say, "Great talking to you. Loved hearing about your new project. I'll call you with my colleague's name, probably tomorrow."

Bob Burg gives some great advice for later in the event. He says, "Check back in with the people you've met. Show them you remember their names. Introduce them to someone who they may find interesting." I would add, "Have an idea for them."

When you introduce people to each other, tell them what a good lead it looks like for each. This will impress both of them and help them get their relationship started.

BC: Are there people at most business events with whom you want to make sure you connect?

LW: On the one hand, I believe everyone is a feature story, everyone is deserving of our highest attention. On the other hand, there are centers of influence in every arena, and good networkers figure out who they are: the leaders in your trade associations, the top sales reps in your industry or company, the people on the board of directors of a volunteer group you're involved with.

This point deserves to be emphasized. Bob Burg calls centers of influence BPOC (big people on campus). He says, "Discover who these people are and do all you can to meet them." I suggest you set a goal for yourself every time you go to a business event to meet at least three centers of influence. These people may or may not become prospects, but they quite likely can become referral alliances. Make a connection with them that will give you a reason to call them later. You want to find ways to serve these influential people as quickly as possible, in any way you can. In a genuine way, earn their liking and trust. Most successful people like to help others; they understand the principle of service. Tell them you are trying to build your business and you could use their help.

At worst, these people can be sources of good advice and direction, introducing you to other centers of influence. At best, they can become incredible customers and referral allies for you, providing a constant supply of referrals.

Dr. Thomas Stanley, author of *Networking with the Affluent* (Irwin, 1996), says, "High-caliber networkers focus their efforts. They first target those who will give the greatest return. Directly analogous to this networking approach is a military example where an attack on an enemy group is focused on the leader of that group. The strategy has an immediate and profound psychological effect on the remaining members of the enemy group and makes it easier to eliminate many of the remaining affinity group." Certainly I'm not suggesting you "take out" centers of influence. However, if you find a way to serve them, many others will fall into line.

BC: Lynne, could you give us some reminder questions that we can ask ourselves after an event, to evaluate how well we did for ourselves?

LW: Sure, Bill. Here are a few things to ask yourself after each networking or business event:

   1. Did I meet my goal for the number of people I wanted to meet?

2. Did I listen actively and generously?

3. Did I find ways to extend the event beyond the event?

4. Did I get there early to help out or talk to the centers of influence?

5. Am I ready to follow up with people promptly— to do what I said I would do?

6. Did I volunteer in a way that would show off my talents or help me learn new skills?

(And a couple of mine:)

7. Did I step out of my comfort zone to meet new people and have genuine conversations with them?

8. Did I have an attitude of giving? Was I looking for ways to give first?

Ten Commandments of Networking

by Dr. Ivan Misner

1. Have your networking tools with you at all times.

Informative name badge, plenty of business cards, brochures, and a pocket-sized business-card file that has the cards of the professionals you prefer.

2. Set a goal for the number of people you'll meet.

Some people go to a meeting with only one goal in mind: the time they plan to leave! To get the most out of a networking event, don't leave until you've met your quota of people.

3. Act like a host, not a guest.

I've started using this idea, and it really works. How would you act at any type of business event if you were the host? Would you be more outgoing? Would you be in a giving mode? Would you watch for lulls in conversations and introduce people to each other? Act like the host and you'll make more quality contacts. Or actually get involved in the organization and host an event.

4. Ask the five Ws: Who, what, where, when, and why.

Don't just skate on the surface with people you meet. Use this simple guideline as a reminder to create quality conversations.

5. Give a lead or referral whenever possible.

6. Describe your product or service.

After learning about your contact, describe your product or service in a way that shows how you truly benefit others.

Ten Commandments
of Networking

7. **Exchange business cards with the people you meet.**

8. **Spend ten minutes or less with each person you meet and don't linger with friends and associates.**

    Although we want to make as many contacts as possible, this advice may need to be adjusted to each individual. If I make a great face-to-face contact at a business event, ten minutes may not be enough time. If you meet someone who could be an incredible referral ally, invest whatever time is appropriate. Be mindful of their needs at this event. If you sense their goal is to meet a lot of people, don't hold them back.

    Don't get stuck in the comfort zone of your friends and associates. Spend a significant amount of the time meeting new people.

9. **Write comments on the backs of the business cards you collect.**

    I write a few reminders to myself: how I can serve them, something they said they would do for me, their hobbies or special interests I discovered. This way, when I get back to my office I can better recall the conversations and take the appropriate action.

10. **Follow up with the people you meet.**

    Good follow-up is the lifeblood of networking. You can obey the previous nine commandments religiously, but if you don't follow up effectively, you're wasting your time!

CHAPTER 12

Stay in Touch with Your Network

BC: How do I decide if I want to add a new contact to my network?

LW: I know that some experts say just work on building your relationships with movers and shakers. I say that everybody is important. The guy who's unemployed today could be the one who starts his own company tomorrow and places a million-dollar order with you in five years. So don't be shortsighted in how you build your network.

BC: After I've met someone new, when should I follow up and what should I do to enhance the relationship?

LW: Remember, the highest forms of networking are teaching and trusting. So, focus on reconnecting in ways that help you learn about them and teach them about you. One restaurant supplies salesperson I coached said to a desktop publisher he met and liked, "How about giving me a short tour of your operation next week? Then when my company needs any graphic arts, I can suggest you." Another example: Mary remembered that Gloria had mentioned the challenge of fitting exercise into her too-busy life. Mary reconnected with a phone call, saying she planned to walk on her lunch hour three times a week and would love a partner.

Find a way to serve these people you meet in any way you can. Help them fix a problem or find an opportunity, no matter how small it may seem. After you've served them, they will be much more receptive to being taught about your business and how they might help you.

Even if the meeting at the event didn't create a specific reason to call back, I try to call every person with whom I had a *significant* encounter within a day or two. Either I have something specific to give them or I clarify who they are and what they do and make sure they're clear about me. When appropriate, I try to set an appointment to explore possibilities.

When I meet an actual prospect at an event and can think of something appropriate, I send them something non-sales-related, something other than my brochure. This will show them that I am interested in more than just selling them something or using them for referrals. I'm interested in a mutually beneficial relationship.

BC: I've heard you say that not all conversations count as effective follow-up. What do you mean by that?

LW: If you're not learning something about them, or teaching them something about you, it doesn't count as follow-up. Talking about the weather and the ball scores may fill some time, but it rarely builds relationships.

BC: In your book, *52 Ways,* you offer some really great follow-up ideas. Could you share a few?

LW: Our 52 ways are coded according to how much time and money they take and whether they will put you in touch with one, a few, or many people. One I like is to watch for advertisements your contacts place and other promotions in which they engage. If it's an ad, you can clip it and mail it to your contact with a complimentary note, or even an idea for new markets. Another idea is to fax ten contacts the copy for a new brochure you're working on and ask for their reactions. This teaches them about you, gathers valuable insight for you, and keeps the relationship active.

A third idea is to set up a brown-bag or catered lunch with a local speaker you'd like to hear and invite a few contacts to join you.

I heard recently of a successful salesperson who has created a reputation for sending his clients, prospects, and networking allies vacation photos that he turns into personal postcards. He takes such funny and creative photos that everyone on his list looks forward to *his* next vacation.

BC: In your book you talk about trust busters and trust builders. Could you explain?

LW: You don't sell products and services. You sell your competence and character. Competence means gearing your conversations to teach people about the excellent job you do, the awards you've won, the way you continue to learn. Character means showing people, moment by moment, that you are fair and honest, will make good on any mistakes, and act with integrity in all your dealings. In every conversation people have with you, they are assessing this. I'm not saying you should go around bragging. Just be certain that when you communicate with others, your competence and character show through.

BC: Do you have any final ideas you'd like to share with us?

LW: One way to assess how you're doing at building a circle of contacts (a network) is to ask yourself once a week, "Who do I have to thank this week?" Reconnect by thanking people who've contributed in any way at all to your success that week—with support, information, resources, ideas, referrals. Give them a call, fax them a note, send flowers, offer to help them. Find a way to acknowledge their help. What a great way to spend Friday afternoon! If you've got at least five people to thank, give yourself a pat on the back. I truly believe that as our capacity for gratitude grows, our ability to give grows. And givers always make a great connection.

As the founder of Business Networks International, Ivan Misner could be called the king of networking organizations. I'd like to end this section on networking by sharing an excerpt from his book. He reports on a study by Robert Davis at the University of San Francisco that concludes that participants in networking groups develop networking skills that the average business professional does not.

Misner says, "The longer I am in the group, the better at networking and the more referrals I get. In addition, it seems that the more referrals I get, the higher the percentage that I close! By developing long-term relationships, I am gaining the trust of the other members, which makes it easier to receive and close the referrals that are passed to me."

Networking at events is one of the fastest ways to find referral alliances who will help you build your business as you help them build theirs. And remember, networking is much more than just going to events. It means creating mutually beneficial relationships that need to be nurtured over time.

SECTION 4

The Third Cornerstone

Prospect for Referrals

CHAPTER 13

People Want to Give You Referrals

If you're in sales, you know that the only way to influence people is to show what's in it for them. Well, what's in it for them to give you referrals? I see two main motivations.

First, your referral source has an opportunity to be a real hero to one or more friends or colleagues. If working with you truly has been a pleasure, he or she can look good by helping a friend or colleague learn about you. When you ask a referral ally, you may be giving that alliance another opportunity to serve one of his or her prospects or customers. Your ally may want to call the customer or prospect first, not only to clear the way for the referral (great for you!), but also to make another helping contact (good for them!). Gloria Gault Geary, a successful professional speaker, says, "I bring up my request for referrals as a *service* to my customers. I give them the opportunity to help their friends and colleagues by telling them about me. It works!"

The second reason for customers to give you referrals is that they want to help you. Don't ever discount the power of this. In fact, I think it is the more powerful reason. If you have been serving them well, most customers will derive great pleasure from helping you become more successful. You just have to ask!

When Do You Ask for Referrals?

You can ask for referrals from anyone—a prospect, a customer, or a referral ally—anytime you've served them; notice I said served them, not *sold* them. Delivering value of any kind counts. Of course, they must recognize that you have given them value. Sometimes they'll come right out and tell you they're pleased. Sometimes you have to ask.

As with most things in life, timing is everything. As a salesperson, you are constantly using your experience and your intuition to determine when and how to use your selling strategies. The same holds true for asking for referrals.

Obviously, the best time to ask customers for referrals is after they've expressed satisfaction with your product or service. But you should also ask your customers periodically, even if the request is not tied to a specific transaction. Most of your customers meet new people all the time, so you want to ask for referrals again and again (without becoming a pest).

You must make serving your referral alliances a high priority. Refer people to them, help them gain information, do whatever you can to help them experience more success. The more you can serve them, the more they will want to serve you with an endless chain of high-quality referrals. With your customers, it is perfectly natural to ask for referrals after a successful transaction. With your referral alliances, that may not always be appropriate. This is where your intuition comes into play. Sometimes it may feel just right for you to serve your referral alliances and then ask for referrals, and sometimes it will seem as if you gave only to get. Generally speaking, I like to ask my alliances for referrals during a separate conversation. Once you have established good relationships, you won't even have to ask very often. They will simply call you when they have someone for you.

What Does It Take to Serve Them?

Most salespeople have the hardest time asking for referrals from their prospects—people they feel they have not yet served. That's why it's so important to find ways to serve your prospects as soon as you can, even ways that have nothing to do with what you sell. For instance, I know a printing salesperson named Gary who called on a high-quality prospect. This prospect liked Gary and seemed inclined to do business with him. But at the moment she needed a printer who could print a special type of label that Gary's company could not produce. Gary found a printer who could serve his prospect, and she was very grateful. Because Gary had planted the seed that he worked from referrals (and accented that concept by referring someone to her) she called him with three hot referrals, and she eventually became a customer as well.

It's important to find ways to serve your prospects as soon as you can, even with ways that have nothing to do with what you sell.

Suppose you sell financial services. Can you serve your prospects before you ever sell them? Of course you can. If you structure it carefully, your first appointment with prospects should help them gain so much perspective on their financial situation that they feel you have served them, even before they give you any business.

If you sell life insurance, use some type of fact finder to accumulate information that puts you in a position to offer the best products and serve your prospects by getting them to take a comprehensive look at an area they may not have considered. Serving them this way will serve you in two ways. First, they begin to like and trust you more, so they are more likely to buy from you. Second, they want to share the value you have brought to them with their friends, family members, and colleagues.

If you sell copiers, educate your prospects by bringing them up to date on the latest copier technology. They will feel served before they are sold.

I have a friend who has built a highly successful roofing business. He likes to establish trust by educating his prospects so they make the best decisions. He knows they can get a great job from other roofers, but after he educates them without pressure, they tend to just sign on with him.

Another way to serve your prospects is to ask what I call *high-gain questions*. These are questions that probe a little and get your prospects thinking about their situation in ways they may not have previously considered. You can ask them to evaluate, compare, or speculate. If you ask a prospect a question and she says, "Well, I've never thought of that before," then you know you've asked a high-gain question. You serve prospects when you get them thinking.

When you serve your prospects on the first appointment, it demonstrates the responsive service they can continue to expect from you. They can see that you are there to help them in any way you can, not just to sell them.

Burt Dubin, a professional speaker and writer who coaches people on building their business from referrals, says, "If the prospect had a valid reason not to buy, and if you earned his respect, then there's no reason for him not to help you." Dubin suggests you say something like, "If you were me, who would you call on next?" If the prospect gives you a name, write it down and ask, "Why did you pick him (her)?" This will lead you into upgrading the referral, which I will cover shortly.

The Three Keys to Asking Prospects for Referrals

The three keys to asking prospects for referrals are:
1. Serve them before you sell them.
2. Plant seeds that you are building your business from referrals.
3. When the rapport is good, ask them directly for referrals.

In his article "Is Your Networking?," sales trainer Dennis Fox writes, "Not every sale is finalized during the first or second appointment. In fact, many times the sales process is a long-term one, taking months or even years to be consummated. Certainly during that time you have many opportunities to gain the confidence, trust, and respect of your prospect in order to ask for a referral. Not only that, a completed sale to a referred client can strengthen the resolve of the potential buyer who referred you in the first place."

Kim, a salesperson in Baltimore, pursued a prospect for several months. Most of her prospecting activity with him was spent playing phone tag. When she finally reached the prospect, she learned that he and his company were moving out of state. This move excluded them from doing business together, but during the conversation rapport was high. So Kim became proactive and asked for a referral. She received three referrals, and two became customers within a month.

The rapport must be right for you to ask people for referrals. They must like you and trust you before they will entertain such a request. I have met some prospects whom I felt comfortable asking for referrals right away, but with a few long-term customers the request still would not be well received.

Be Flexible

In *Relationship Selling*, Jim Cathcart describes various communication styles. As you become more aware of the various styles, you can become more flexible with your style and build greater rapport right from the start. One parameter of communication he discusses is *open* versus *contained*.

Open people talk about their feelings and let others talk about feelings. They let people into their lives easily. You may call a prospect for the first time, hoping for five minutes of her time. The next thing you know you've been on the phone for 20 minutes. You know where her kids go to school, why she's mad at her boss today, and much more. Ask an open person a closed-ended question, and you'll still get an open-ended answer. Open people are usually much easier to gain an appointment with than contained people.

Contained people reveal information only when it serves a specific purpose. They operate on a need-to-know basis. They are usually uncomfortable sharing their feelings. They let new people into their lives slowly and only on their terms. Ask a contained person an open-ended question and you'll get a closed-ended answer. ("What types of printing do you buy?" "All kinds.") Unless a contained person has an explicit need for what you sell and is in a buying posture, it usually takes several contacts to gain an appointment.

What does this have to do with asking for referrals? As you might surmise, open people will feel much more comfortable with a request for referrals, much sooner, than contained people. The more contained your prospect or customer, the more you need to wait for substantial rapport and trust to develop. I've made the mistake of asking moderately contained people for referrals too soon, and it was painfully clear they were not ready. This doesn't mean you never ask them for referrals. It just means you must take a little more time and care in building the relationship.

Target Niche Markets

Section Five of the book discusses the benefits and techniques of targeting niche markets. When you target an industry, you gain much knowledge of that industry and how your various customers handle different challenges. When you call on prospects in your target industry, your knowledge and experience bring much value to them. You can discuss issues they are facing that another salesperson would not be familiar with. You can bring them ideas and perspectives that serve them, even before you sell them.

Targeting niche markets sets up opportunities for you to deliver value right away—even before you complete a sale.

The Goal Is Still Making the Sale

Now, in all this discussion about service, I don't mean to diminish the importance of making the sale. That's still paramount—but when you serve your prospects from the very beginning, the sale becomes much easier.

The better you serve your customers, referral alliances, and prospects, the higher the quality of referrals you will get. They will take a stake in your success by giving you a steady supply of referrals.

CHAPTER 14

How to Ask for Referrals

Once you have adopted the mindset that you are building your business from referrals, you want to let everyone know, as soon and as often as possible, without being obnoxious.

Start by Planting Seeds

Just as Johnny Appleseed wandered the countryside planting seeds that sprouted into apple trees, you want to plant referral seeds whenever and wherever you can. Never miss an opportunity to let people know you work from referrals.

When you are with a prospect, even on the first appointment, you might say, "Lynne, I'm building my business by referrals. Which means to you that I will give you the best service I can. I want to earn the right to talk to you about whom you know who also might benefit from our services. I know if you are pleased with the work we do you'll be willing to have such a conversation. "The *feature* here is that I work off of referrals; the *benefit* to the prospect is great service. This plants the seed for referrals while making a strong benefit statement. How you say this doesn't matter. Use your own words. But use the concept of planting seeds.

Lynne Schwabe sows seeds to grow her business all the time. "We always make it clear from the beginning of a relationship with a customer that we build our business by referrals and therefore customer service and high-quality performance are very important to us."

Whenever you talk with your customers or your referral alliances, mention the referrals you've gotten and how you just met someone from a referral, whatever you can fit into the conversation. This way you remind them of how important referrals are to you, without bugging them. If you are serving them and your relationship well, they will be happy to help you when they can. You just have to remind them from time to time, and in different ways.

I'll bet you've had a few prospects volunteer referrals to you without your even asking. It's great, isn't it? Now discover what will happen for you as you become a little more proactive.

Plant seeds in your written correspondence and promotional literature as well: "94% of Bill's clients are obtained through referrals, because they like his work and trust him enough to recommend him to their friends and colleagues." I just met a sales coach named Ramon who has "BY REFERRAL ONLY" printed on his business cards. It's a great idea; I think I'm going to do the same.

If all you add to your selling toolbox is this seed-planting technique, I guarantee that you will receive more referrals from prospects and customers. This one simple technique can contribute to a significant increase in your sales.

Foreshadow Your Request

The feature/benefit seed-planting example is also an example of foreshadowing. Let me explain this technique with an illustration from the movie industry.

Screenwriters and directors employ the device of foreshadowing quite often. Some seemingly insignificant event happens early in the movie that turns out to tie into a very significant event later. This foreshadowing of something to come is used for two main purposes. First, it sets up *expecta-*

tions—and the movie had better deliver. (Anton Chekhov, the master playwright, said, "If you show the audience a gun in Act One, someone had better fire it by Act Three.") Second, foreshadowing can help make something that happens more *believable.*

The better the screenwriter and director, the less likely you will consciously notice the foreshadowing.

So in the sales process, we can use foreshadowing to set up expectations for some future event. We let our prospects and customers know that, at some point, we may ask them for referrals. Then when we do ask, it's easier for us to ask, and it's easier for them to hear.

This foreshadowing technique can be applied to other aspects of the sale as well. If there is any part of the selling process that makes you uncomfortable, you can help yourself with foreshadowing.

I was working with a residential remodeling company, teaching architects some selling skills. These architects were to move their prospects through a series of small commitments that would eventually result in the sale, and they were having difficulty moving the process along effectively.

I suggested that the first time they meet with a prospect, they spell out the entire process: "First, if you like what we discuss this evening, I will ask you for permission to work up some preliminary drawings for the addition to your home. Our fee for that is $500. If you like what you see, the next step is to move into the more complete set of plans. Our fee for that is. . . ." And so on. By telling the prospect exactly what was to come, the architects could much more easily bring up the subject of increasing the commitment. All they had to say was, "Do you remember what I told you our next step would be?" ("To draw up the more complete set of plans?") "That's right. Well, now it's that time. Shall we go for it?"

Watch yourself to see when you hit what my colleague Dave Sandler called *Wimp Junction*—that place where you need to ask an important question but you usually wimp out. We all pass through Wimp Junction every day. Sometimes we are courageous and move through the fear to the bold action, and sometimes we wimp out. Use foreshadowing to help you move through the parts of the sales that put you face to face with Wimp Junction. Mark Sheer (*Referrals*) recommends sending a letter to customers and referral alliances to warm them up to the fact that you will be asking them for referrals. Mark mails this letter with his client profile, which we will cover soon.

My Three-Step Approach To Asking for Referrals

Step 1: Treat asking for referrals with reverence.

Don't ask for a referral on your way out the door by saying, "Oh, by the way, do you know anyone else I can call?" No! When and how you ask will demonstrate that this is important to you. You need to be sure you can set aside at least five to 10 minutes of your referral source's time.

The approach that works best for me is, "Lynne, I have something important I've been meaning to ask you." This is guaranteed to get her attention.

Some salespeople like to make a warm-up statement before they ask for referrals: "We've been doing business together for about a year. And from what you've told me, you've been pleased with our performance." This is fine. Just don't make this warm-up too long or convoluted. When salespeople role-play these techniques in my workshops, they often go on and on, probably because this is new to them and they feel a bit awkward. Warm it up a little if you need to, but get to the asking quickly!

Step 2: Ask for their help.

The most powerful words you can use in asking for referrals are, "I need your help." If you've served your customer, referral alliance, or prospect well, if you've built rapport and trust, then he or she will be happy to give you referrals. You just have to ask.

How many times have you stopped to ask strangers for directions, and they went out of their way to help you? It happens to me all the time. Sometimes they'll draw a map. Sometimes they'll offer to lead the way in their car. I've even had people offer to get in my car and direct me. Just think what you can get if you *ask* for referrals!

In *Sell and Grow Rich* (Dearborn Financial Publishing, 1993), Joe Gandolfo tells of how he learned to prospect for referrals from a paint salesman. "After I had been selling for a few years, I called upon a prospect. While in his apartment I saw plaques and trophies all over. Here's the conversation we had:

JG: What are these plaques and trophies for?

Paint Salesman: I won them for being the top paint sales-man in the United States.

JG: How did you become number one?

PS: Because I know the magic words.

JG: What magic words?

PS: I say, 'I need your help.' When you ask for help, no one ever says no.

JG: What help do you ask for?

PS: I ask for the names of three friends.

Step 3: Get permission to explore or brainstorm whom they know, and limit their field of view.

When you use a weak phrase like, "Do you know anyone . . . ?" you're asking too broad a question, and you haven't gained permission to help your source think. If he hesitates for just a little, since you're probably feeling awkward anyway, you'll bail out too soon (Wimp Junction). You'll say something like, "Well, that's OK. If you think of anyone, just give me a call." Don't do that to yourself. If he says, "Well, I can't think of anyone offhand," then you're really dead in the water.

You deserve to get more, and you can! When you gain permission to explore or brainstorm, you can help your sources come up with names. You can have a brief conversation about it.

The statement might go something like this: "I was wondering, with your permission, if we could brainstorm for a second on whom you know that might be able to benefit from the same working relationship we've been able to establish. Is that all right?"

When she says "yes" and then hesitates, you can help explore for a few minutes. The better your relationship, and the braver you feel, the more likely you will keep exploring.

Be patient. After your request, she may need a minute to shift her brain to it. Ask, and then be OK with the silence. If you see her struggling, then you can begin to gently assist the process.

If you are targeting a niche market (discussed in Section Five), you might consider pulling out a list of industry influencers you are trying to reach. Perhaps your source knows one of them. Or you might ask her to open up her membership directory.

Let's sum up what we've covered so far by putting the statements together. In the following dialogue, SP is the salesperson and RS is the referral source (prospect, alliance, or customer).

SP: Dave, I'm glad we've been able to serve you once again. I have an important question I've been meaning to ask you."

RS: "OK, shoot."

SP: "I'm building my business, and I need your help."

RS: "What can I do?"

SP: "Well, with your permission, I was wondering if we could explore for a second whom you know who I should be calling on.

RS: "OK, let me think . . ."

SP: "I know you're active in your association. Of the people you know there, who are the two or three I should be calling?" (Or: "I know you are active in your association. If you were me, who would you call?")

Explore and Brainstorm

There are many ways to explore or brainstorm. The more you've worked on establishing a great relationship with your customers, the more you will know about them. The more you know about them, the more you can participate in the exploration.

Of course, it also depends on what you are selling. If you are selling life insurance, you might try to connect with just about any adult. If you are selling printing, you want to look for other print buyers—places your sources worked before, classmates from graphic arts school, places where their fellow employees have moved, and so on. They can also lead you to other referral alliances.

Focus on your industry and list all the possible avenues of exploration you might pursue with your customers. Then when you receive permission to explore, you're ready to go.

The exact words you use in the exploration (or brainstorming) don't matter as much as the fact that they are genuine and that you begin to focus your sources' thinking a bit so they can begin to *picture* specific people in their minds.

You can ask whom they know who might be a likely candidate to purchase your product or service, or you can take a different approach and ask who they know who might benefit from the same working relationship you've been able to establish. Remember our discussion about open and contained individuals? With individuals who are more open, I usually try the "relationship" approach. With more contained people, I recommend the "product/service" approach. Use your best judgment and do what you think will be most effective. About once a year, my life insurance agent, Haig, takes me out to lunch to update my policy and to pick my brain for referrals. The first two or three times we did this, I brought along membership directories for several associations to which I belong.

Many of your customers and referral alliances will open their directories up to you and tell you about whom they know. If you are targeting their industry, all the better. If you schedule a referral gathering lunch (or even if you don't), don't be afraid to ask them to look through whatever directories they have.

Some sales coaches tell you to get as many names as possible in one sitting. I suggest you go for three to five solid referrals. Upgrade them the best you can at that session (more on this in a minute) and follow them through to their natural conclusion. Then go back for more. If you get too many names in one sitting, the referrals may not be as well thought out or as high quality.

Variations on exploring

1. After you gain permission to explore or brainstorm, but before you actually do it, you can put your source more at ease with the referral process by explaining how you will go about contacting anyone who is referred to you. Assure her that if her friend or colleague has no interest in what you are selling, you'll back off immediately. This will show her that your approach will be soft and professional.

2. To ease the tension that you may feel in this asking process, you can interject some fun by asking for 100 names. You'll both chuckle for a second. Then when you ask for three names, your request will seem small by comparison, yet it will yield more than just one name.

Collect the Names First

As your source gives you a name, write it down. Don't ask anything else about this person quite yet. You want to give him the space to come up with other names. After the first name you might say, "Great. Anyone else come to mind?" Once he's finished giving you names, then you can go back and learn about these individuals.

I've had some customers open their Rolodexes and their association directories for me. I'll usually go for the top three to five and ask my source if I can come back later for more. Because I'm so busy delivering speeches and seminars, I can't prospect (and don't need to as much anymore, thank goodness) too many people at one time. Your situation may be different. You may have a short sell cycle and/or you may need to do more prospecting. If you are new at what you are selling, you probably want to go for as many names as possible. But before you call all those names, make sure you read Chapter 15 on upgrading referrals and warming up prospects.

Don't Let Your Referral Source Prequalify Your New Prospects

Scott Kramnick, author of *Expecting Referrals* (Associates Publishing, 1993), writes, "Quite often your customers will prequalify the referrals in their head before giving you names. This is not usually good for you. Let them know that you work with a wide range of situations, and that they shouldn't assume. . . ." This illustrates the importance of helping your customers and referral alliances learn of all that you do and how you benefit customers. If there is any qualifying going on, you want to be a part of it.

A colleague of mine, and great professional speaker, David Rich, wanted me to tell you that to be powerful in asking for referrals, you need to get to know your customers, prospects, and referral alliances as well as possible. When you have a sense of who they are and how they spend their time, you can explore or brainstorm with them much more effectively.

As I discussed earlier, it's important to get to know your customers in ways that have nothing to do with what you're selling them. This puts you in a position to help them in many other ways. People do business with people they like and trust. People give referrals to people they like and trust. Really getting to know your customers will help build these important qualities in your relationships.

Use a Client Profile

Mark Sheer says the best way to keep the exploration (or brainstorming) alive is by sharing your client profile with your referral source. Sheer says, "Everyone must develop a visual Client Profile, which includes: who you can help, what problems you can solve, and how you can help others reach their goals. To obtain referrals that will expand your business and increase profits, you must ask what *they* need and show what *you* need."

Basically, he suggests that you come up with a written document you can use to stimulate the exploration with your referral source. I've seen others use this approach. Some actually hand the document over to the source, while others just use it as a jumping-off point for questions.

On the back of the brochure Sheer uses to promote his sales seminars is his own client profile:

> I'm expanding my business and need your help.
> WHO DO YOU KNOW WHO . . .
>
> ■ Wants to expand their business, is goal oriented, and wants to increase production?
> ■ Has ten or more salespeople?
> ■ Has award meetings, large sales meetings, or conventions?
> ■ Can introduce me to the person who makes decisions?

Sheer illustrates how to use the client profile to ask open-ended questions. He says that if you are asking for referrals but not getting them, you are probably asking closed-ended questions. Sheer asks, "Do you use closed-ended questions such as, 'Do you know someone who needs to refinance their home loan?'

"Using this close-ended, limited approach encourages that contact to respond with minimal thinking, 'Well, no one has said that they need to refinance, so I'll say—NO.'

"You respond, 'Oh, okay, Thanks anyway.'

"And the conversation is over."

How you ask for referrals can set you up to hit Wimp Junction. Let's continue with Sheer's example.

To bypass the automatic *no*, Sheer advises an open-ended approach. His examples:

> "I'm expanding my business and I need your help. Who do you know who has recently had a baby?"
>
> "Who do you know who is getting ready to retire?"
>
> "Who do you know who mentioned that their retirement plan may not be adequate and is worried about it?"

While I agree that open-ended questions are a major part of a salesperson's toolbox, closed-ended questions also have their place, even in asking for referrals. For instance, if you are dealing with one of those contained individuals we've discussed, he or she may feel much more comfortable with closed-ended questions. Unless you know the source well, you may be better off in the rapport department with a more restricted exploration process. Read your audience, and respond in kind.

Get to know your customers in ways that have nothing to do with what you're selling them.

You may already know that your source knows some perfect prospects for you. If the rapport is good, ask directly if he or she can refer you to them.

Take time to create a client profile to help you explore for referrals. This profile is basically a list of all the types of people who are good prospects for you: people you can help, people who have needs you can meet, people who have problems you can solve.

Stop reading for a minute. Get out a piece of paper and start your client profile. Even if you never formalize the profile, this exercise will strengthen your ability to explore and brainstorm.

Upgrade the Referral and Warm Up Your Prospect

Once you've been given a referral, you could call your new prospect and probably get off to a good start. In this chapter I'll show you some strategies to make sure your first contact with the new prospect is as effective as possible, right from the beginning.

Upgrade the Referral

Scott Kramnick defines three levels of referrals. I've adjusted his model to distinguish among four levels.

Level 1

This is a really a cold referral. You've been given a name and phone number, but you can't use the referral source's name. This lead will only produce a well-targeted cold call. Depending on the stage of your career or the potential of this prospect, you may still want to make the call. But unless this prospect has an explicit need for what you are selling, you'll probably get the cold shoulder. Now your cold-call selling skills will come into play.

Level 2

> This is a lukewarm referral. You have the name and number, and you do have permission to use your referral source's name. Now you have a good shot at getting past this prospect's knee-jerk reaction and into a conversation. When a referral source gives you a referral, always ask for permission to use his or her name. This is a common courtesy and can sometimes be revealing.

Level 3

> This is a warm referral. You have the above, plus some information about the prospect and/or the prospect's company. Unfortunately, too many salespeople settle for Level 2 referrals. The only information they get is what their referral source volunteers. They get a name, number, and permission, and then say, "Thanks for the referral. I'll give her a call right away." Such a waste!
>
> What might you like to know about your new prospect? Here are a few questions you should consider asking. (You might think of some more, relevant to your world.)
>
> 1. How do you know this person? What is the nature of your relationship?
> 2. What is his or her job title or exact position in the company?
> 3. What can you tell me about his or her business?
> 4. What type of personality am I likely to encounter? Is this person direct? Is she very open, or contained?
> 5. Does he have any hobbies or special interests?
> 6. Why do you think we will be a good match? Is there anything we seem to have in common?
> 7. What are some of the challenges she is facing in general, or related to my product/service?
>
> These are the types of things you can't learn from directories or other lists of prospects (cold research). This warm research can come only from referrals.

Level 4

This is a *hot* referral. You know all of the above and you learn they have a very specific need for what you sell. Obviously, this is the best place to be in the sales process.

Whatever level your source takes you to, your job is to warm it up. The extent to which you can upgrade your referrals depends on at least two things:

1. The relationship you've been able to establish with your source. The better the relationship, the more willing your source will be to cooperate.

2. Your courage. Wimp Junction can become a factor here. Once you've done it a few times, it will get easier.

IMPORTANT! If you've discovered your prospect has a problem or an explicit need, you want to ask your source for advice on how to proceed. For example, "How do you think Mary will react to our discussing some of her problems? Can I bring them up, or should I be less direct?" Your source will coach you on the best course of action here. You want your new prospect to feel comfortable about her name coming up in conversation. Remember, referral selling is all about building and *protecting* relationships. This should also work for hobbies or any other personal information you've gathered. If your referral source advises against bringing it up directly, think of some questions that might elicit the information. Example: "I just worked with a client who had a problem with delivery. Is that something you've ever experienced?"

Let's say you obtained a name from your source, but you could tell that his time was running too short to upgrade the referral. No problem! You can call him later that day or the next day and upgrade it some more. I've been given referrals, upgraded them briefly at that time, and then called my source later to gather more information. You might say, "Dave, thanks again for giving me Mary's number. I was about to give her a call and I realized we didn't really know much about each other. It would be better for both of us if I could gain a little more information." It's never too late to upgrade the referral.

Sales trainer Dennis Fox suggests that if you get several names from your referral source, ask, "Who should I contact first?" or "If you were me, who would you call first?" Then ask why. This will get your source into the upgrading process smoothly and naturally.

Top life insurance salesperson Robert Kerrigan recommends learning as much as possible about your referral prospect for two reasons. You will be able to create more commonality to warm up the conversation. And, he says, "The more you know about your prospect, the more they become a real person to you, the more you can become truly enthusiastic about calling them." Your enthusiasm for them will come across and help you build rapport right from the start.

Warm Up the Prospect Before You Call

At this point you could call your new prospect and probably have a warm call with pretty good results. Or you could warm it up some more to increase the likelihood of good results. Here are seven great ways you can warm up your referral prospects.

Warm-up 1: Referral source writes a note on your brochure.

If I have one of my brochures with me, I may pull it out and ask my referral source to write a quick note to the prospect, right on the brochure. Now the brochure is personalized for the prospect.

Warm-up 2: Referral source adds a PS to your letter.

Sometimes, and this works great, I'll have a brief conversation with the souce such as the following:

Me: Dave, I think what I'll do first before I call Mary is send her a letter letting her know that her name came up in conversation. I'll mention

a little about what I do and how I've served
you, and then tell her I'll follow up with a
phone call. I was hoping I could send you the
letter first, with a pre-addressed and stamped
envelope. If it looks OK to you, you can send it
on. Would that be OK?

Dave: Yes.

Me: Tell you what, I'll leave space for a PS where
you can write a quick personal note to Mary.
She might appreciate that. Would that be OK?

I've never had anyone turn me down. Research has
shown that the PS is a very powerful part of a letter, and
your PS is a personal note from your referral source.
Could you ask for a more effective warm-up letter?

**Warm-up 3: Create special stationery for your referral source
and have him or her send a personal note.**

Here's an idea I got from my life insurance agent, Haig.
At our annual lunch, we talked about my needs in his
areas of expertise and then we talked referrals. As usual,
I had four or five decent referrals for him. Instead of
just offering to call these prospects, I waited to see what
warm-up method he would choose (if any). He pulled
out some stationary he had created with my name on
it. It was Monarch-size stationery ($6\frac{1}{2}$ by $8\frac{1}{2}$ inches).
He had written a sample letter that I could send to
these prospects before he called. I liked what he had
written but offered to rewrite it in my own words to
make it even more personal. I also liked the personal
feel of the Monarch stationery. So in this case, Haig's
new referral prospects will receive a personal note from
me before he contacts them.

Warm-up 4: Get your source to phone your new prospect.

I use this one the most often these days and find it the
most powerful for normal situations. Get the source to
call the prospect—not as a favor to you, but to help
protect his relationship with his friend or colleague.

At one of the first sales training programs I ever attended, the trainer told us that after we get a referral, we should then ask our customer to call the prospect right on the spot. Having my customer call my prospect sounded great until I tried it. I just couldn't get the words out of my mouth, and I've found very few salespeople who can. The problem with this technique is that you would be asking your customer to call your new prospect as a favor to you. You'd already asked for his help in requesting referrals. This may be stretching it.

You may have customers who will volunteer to call the prospect just to help you. And of course you should let them. In most cases, though, there is another reason why they may want to call their friend or colleague. There is something in it for them: protecting their relationship. Your request might go something like this:

You: Dave, I appreciate your giving me Mary's name. I'll call her in a few days. I'm thinking . . . maybe she would prefer hearing from you before I call, so she knows you gave me her name and she'll be expecting my call. This way I won't be such a stranger. Do you think she might appreciate that?

Dave: That's a good idea, actually. I'll do that.

You: Sounds good. Let's see, today is Monday; how about I call her Thursday? That should give you a couple of days to reach her. Sound reasonable?

    (Phrase this request in your own words. Just make it genuine.)

I need to emphasize a point here. This is not a request to have your customer or referral alliance call the prospect. Your statement must not begin with "Would you mind calling. . . ." It's stronger when your purpose is to protect their relationship. Here's another way you could word it:

You: Dave, thanks for helping me meet Mary. I was
         wondering . . . maybe she would appreciate
         hearing from you first, just to know that you
         aren't siccing a salesperson on her. Would that
         be appropriate?

Dave: Yes, thanks for mentioning that.

You: Great. Let's see, this is Monday; I'll probably be
         able to call her Thursday. Would that leave you
         enough time to make a quick call?

Dave: I think so.

You: Thanks. You know, I don't want this to be a
         hassle for you. If you get her voice mail, a quick
         message will probably do the trick.

After getting your source's word to call the prospect
in the next couple of days, when you get back to your
office, send a fax or e-mail message: "Thanks for the
meeting and referring me to Mary. When you call
Mary to let her know I'll be calling, you can assure her
that I'll be very professional and will pursue only if she
is interested." This accomplishes two things: it thanks
your referral source (always good to do quickly and
often) and it reminds him of the phone call to which
he committed.

Now you have your satisfied customer or referral
alliance saying good things about you behind your
back. When you call your prospect, she's expecting
your call, she knows why you're calling, and best of all,
she's heard good things about you. Could you ask for a
better start with a new prospect?

If, for whatever reason, your source will not be calling your new prospect, as you are leaving the appointment you might say, "By the way, when I speak to
Mary, I know it's OK to mention your name. If it
makes her feel more comfortable, can I suggest that she
give you a call as a reference?"

Warm-up 5: Take your source and prospect to lunch.

If your referral source and your new prospect are good friends, either professionally or socially, and you get along well with your source, invite the two of them to lunch, dinner, or a business event. You can do this before you actually have an appointment with your new prospect or after the first appointment. Either way, if you can get the two of them together with you, it's pure gold!

Warm-up 6: Attend your source's association meeting.

If you are targeting a niche market and you have a customer or a referral alliance who is somewhat active with the association in your target industry, see if he will take you as a guest to an event (such as their local monthly meeting). Now you have your satisfied customer introducing you, face to face, to new prospects.

Warm-up 7: Create a special warm-up audiotape.

Here's a very creative and powerful idea. I challenge you to use it. If you do, you'll reap great rewards. I use this approach, but I'd rather tell you how someone else is using it effectively.

Jerry Mofield is a very successful American Express Financial Advisor. He's successful because he gives good, sound advice to his clients, he serves them well, and he is a creative salesperson. Jerry uses an audiotape brochure to warm up his new referral prospects.

The audiotape is simply a brief interview with Jerry in which he shares his financial planning philosophy. The tape gives his prospects the opportunity to evaluate Jerry's philosophy and decide whether it matches theirs. But this could be done in a written brochure. The advantage of the audiotape is that it gives his prospects a sense of Jerry's demeanor, something that's hard to convey through the written word. They get a real sense of who Jerry is.

Jerry uses the tape in a very powerful way. He gives every satisfied client at least one copy to share with whomever they choose. His satisfied clients hand the tapes out to their friends and colleagues, and Jerry replenishes their supply. Now Jerry has some very warm prospects to call, and his clients have been supplied with more tapes, to make more referrals.

If, for instance, your referral source didn't want to call the prospect, ask if he would like to send her your audio brochure. Very effective!

CHAPTER 16

Calling Your Prospects

After you've gotten referrals and warmed them up, it's time to call your new prospects. Let me give you one possible opening sequence, and then we'll come back to analyze it.

The Opening Statement

Me: Hello, Ms. Sylvester, this is Bill Cates with ABC Graphics. I know you're busy. The reason I'm calling is that your name came up in conversation with Dave Montgomery with the XYZ Association. Dave said you used to work together, is that right?

Mary: Yes.

Me: Dave has been very pleased with the working relationship we've been able to establish, and since he knows I work mainly from referrals, he was kind enough to give me your name, and thought it was worth a few minutes of our time to see if we should know each other. Am I correct in assuming you're the person I should speak to about your graphic arts services?

Now let's go back and take a closer look.

Analyzing the opening

STEP 1

Identify yourself and your company. Simple.

STEP 2

"I know you're busy. The reason I'm calling . . . " I got
this opener from professional speaker David Rich, CSP.
David taught me that you want to let them know that
you respect their time, and that your time is valuable
too and you have a specific reason for calling. In my
opening statement, I don't want to ask if they are busy,
because what are they going to say? "Yes, I'm busy."
Now you feel the pressure to hurry up, and you usually
bail out too soon. A couple of minutes into the conversation, after you've gotten past any possible knee-jerk
reaction (which rarely happens with referrals), then you
may want to ask, "Is now a good time to start the conversation" Or, "Do you have a minute for this now?"

STEP 3

"Your name came up in conversation with Dave
Montgomery." You mention the referral source's name
and ask a simple closed-ended question. This keeps
your opening statement fairly brief and gives it some
breathing space.

STEP 4

"Dave has been very pleased with the working relationship we've been able to establish. . . ." This is an
optional statement that I like to use because it brings in
the endorsement value of the referral.

STEP 5

"and since he knows I work mainly from referrals, he
was kind enough to give me your name. . . ." This is
seed planting and a prestige builder. First, I want to let
her know soon (and often) that I work from referrals.

Second, the fact that I work from referrals means that I really must serve my customers well.

STEP 6

"Am I correct in assuming you're the person I should speak to about your graphic arts services?" This concludes your opening statement with a question. Your prospect's answer will determine the course you take from here. If you've learned some things about her or her business, and she seems very open to this conversation, you may want to mention some of that now. However, I wouldn't bring up too much all at once. You want to ask good questions, qualify the person a bit, and then go for the appointment. At the appointment, you can bring up other things you may have learned from your referral source.

Remember: If your referral source told you about a problem your prospect was having, first ask your source if it would be OK for you to mention it to your prospect. When in doubt, don't bring it up directly. Instead, ask the prospect a question or two that may elicit the information.

Optional phrases

Here are two optional phrases you can add to your opening statement. Some salespeople find them helpful. Judge for yourself.

Optional phrase #1

"Dave didn't assume that you would want to meet with me. . . ." I got this little statement from Rick Hill. He says, and I've found it's true, that this statement takes the pressure off your prospect. There are two types of pressures your prospect may be feeling: 1) the pressure some people feel whenever a sales person calls, and 2) pressure because they know your referral source and don't want to damage the relationship in any way. Saying, "Dave didn't assume . . ." or something similar goes a long way to warm up the conversation.

Also, many prospects have difficulty saying no. They string you along with a lot of fuzzy phrases. This phenomenon, which I'm sure you've experienced, can be compounded when you reach this type of prospect from a referral. When they learn that you know their friend or colleague, they may have even more difficulty telling you the truth. If you sense this is happening, don't be afraid to go for the "no." Then let go. If the rapport is good, ask for referrals.

Optional phrase #2

Particularly if you are selling a service (such as consulting, accounting, or any other ongoing kind of service relationship) you may want to base this conversation on the great working relationship you and your customer have been able to establish. Example: "Dave was pleased with the working relationship we've been able to establish and thought you'd like to explore how I might be able to make your life a little easier as well."

Keep Your Referral Source Posted

Tell your source when you think you will be contacting the referral. If it will take a few weeks to get to it, let your source know this. If he speaks to your new prospect before you do, he won't wonder why you haven't followed through on the help he's given you.

This is an integrity issue. You asked for help. You had better follow through or you may not get any more. Robert Kerrigan says, "People have great respect for integrity demonstrated in small ways."

Once I've contacted my new prospect, I call my referral source to let him know the status and to thank him again. This is important, not just to prove that you are following through, but because you may get more referrals on this call. At worst, you have reminded your customer or referral alliance that you are building your business with referrals.

Thank Your Referral Source

After you receive a referral, send your source a thank-you note or letter that acknowledges the power his referral carries. I recently obtained five referrals from a client. Mentioning her name opened the door for me; I have already done business with three contacts, and the other two still look good. When I called to thank her I said, "You sure are respected out there. All I had to do was mention your name." She was flattered.

Once that referral turns into a sale, send your source a small gift with a note. I like to find one that suits my referral source, perhaps something to do with a hobby. Harvey Mackay suggests the gift should be "thoughtful rather than expensive."

In most cases, it won't be appropriate to pay a commission to a customer who refers you. However, it may be appropriate with some members of your referral alliance to structure a relationship in which you *do* reward each other for referred business.

Generally speaking, I like to help people with referrals as best I can, knowing it will come back to me.

Marilyn Jennings, the most successful real-estate agent in Canada, sends thank-you gifts for specific referrals. And twice a year she sends a rather expensive gift basket to everyone with whom she's had a transaction. She encloses a note of thanks for past business and a reminder that she values the person's referrals. She says this one technique alone, although a significant financial commitment, yields tremendous results. She has used it to build a business that's so successful that she has more real-estate transactions in a month than the average agent has in a year.

CHAPTER 17

Potential Obstacles

If you follow the method that I've given you, the obstacles you encounter will be minimal. However, on occasion, you may encounter obstacles in two places: with your customers, and within yourself.

Customer Obstacles

Here are some common reasons why people may be reluctant or unwilling to give you referrals.

1. They don't like and trust you enough.
2. They don't want to sic a salesperson on a friend or colleague, because they may look down on sales people in general.
3. They aren't clear about what you do and how you might benefit their friend or colleague.
4. They prequalify their friends and colleagues for you even before speaking their names.
5. They are afraid of upsetting their relationships.
6. They don't want to appear that they're talking behind this person's back.

7. They may believe in the product or service, but don't like the salesperson.

8. They can't think of anyone.

9. They truly don't know anyone.

Remember, if you constantly bring value to your customers and create relationships in which they like you and trust you, objections will be rare; people will *want* to help you.

If they don't like or trust you enough, they probably won't tell you so. And there's nothing you can do on the spot except to back off as they continue to resist. Then keep working hard to gain their trust.

Your open customers will usually have no difficulty with your request for referrals. But your contained customers will not appreciate the request too early in the relationship.

If you sense that your customer or friendly prospect is uncomfortable with the request, ask. It might sound like this: "I get the feeling that you may not yet be comfortable with providing me with referrals. Is this the case?" Straight and honest communication, softened with genuine sincerity, is the straightest line to a better relationship. Asking this question will usually give rise to a good conversation that, even if it does not result in referrals, will still strengthen your relationship. It's possible they had a bad experience in the past and need a little reassurance that you won't pester their friend or colleague.

If you sense hesitancy right away, you might say, "Let me tell you what I'm going to do with any names you give me. I will make one phone call to each person, telling them that their name came up in conversation with you. You can even call them first, to let them know why you gave me their name. I'll explore whether there is any reason we should stay in touch. If they express interest, we will get together and I'll give them the same professional service I've given you. If they aren't interested, I will thank them for their time and bow out gracefully."

On occasion, I have prefaced my request for referrals by musing about how we met, how I prospected them, and why they finally decided to do business with me. This reminds them that it was a pleasant experience. Then when I ask for referrals, they don't feel an unconscious fear that they will be siccing a salesperson on one of their friends or colleagues.

I'd like to share with you my formula for exploring any obstacles that might arise with your potential referral sources. This formula can work on almost any stall, objection, or other obstacle a prospect or customer can throw at you during the selling process. I guarantee that if you adopt it, obstacles will be much easier to deal with.

First, you must have the right frame of mind. Many people believe you have to "overcome" objections. I believe that in this day and age, that attitude can hurt you more than help you. When you feel you have to overcome objections, you come from a place where the customer or prospect is wrong, you're right, and you're going to change his or her mind. Most buyers won't stand for that anymore. Their perception is their reality, and you'd better honor it.

> Straight and honest communication, softened with genuine sincerity, is the straightest line to a better relationship.

I suggest that you adopt an attitude of "exploring" obstacles. Sometimes they can be reduced or eliminated, and sometimes they can't. You want to put yourself in position to explore the obstacle to see if it can be eliminated or if you just need to move on. Here are the five steps for exploring obstacles successfully. After the steps, I will show you how they might be used in the referral-gathering process.

Five steps to dealing with customer obstacles

STEP 1

Agree and validate their position: Because your prospects' or customers' perception is their reality, and because they will resist your attempts to change their view, the first and most powerful thing you can do is to validate their position. After you validate their position with some a supporting statement, don't erase that goodwill by using the word "but," which negates everything you said just before it. I urge you to remove *but* from your selling vocabulary and replace it with *and*, which merely adds to what you've said. I'll show you an example in a minute.

STEP 2

Ask permission to explore: You want to fully understand the nature of their resistance and what the deeper truth might be. You need to be soft here. I've found that when I ask permission to explore—have a quick conversation about it—prospects or customers are not threatened and do not get defensive. My soft way into it allows them to feel comfortable and open up a bit more.

STEP 3

Reframe their view of things gently, with their permission: If, in the exploration step, you realize they may be willing to consider other ways to look at things, you want to gently help them do that. If you can accomplish this by educating them further or other quick thinking on your part, move to Step 4. On the other hand, if their resistance is deep rooted, you probably want to move on to Step 5.

STEP 4

Gain agreement and move on with the conversation: In this step, you basically ask if they can see and accept the new "frame" or perspective you've shown them. If they can, then you continue exploring whom they know who may also benefit from knowing you.

STEP 5

If resistance is deep, back off: Because selling is a relationship game (especially when it comes to using referrals), you don't want to weaken your relationships. If a prospect is adamant, you're better off retreating and living to "fight" another day. I've known many salespeople who have asked for referrals, encountered some resistance, backed off, and then received many referrals from that same customer later.

A sample conversation

Here's a sample conversation using this formula (SP is the salesperson; CU is the customer):

CU: I'm not sure I feel comfortable with giving you referrals at this time.

SP: I appreciate that; not everyone is comfortable with this process. Would you mind if we explored that for just a second?

CU: I guess so.

SP: I was wondering, are you uncomfortable with referrals because you had a bad experience with it in the past?

CU: Actually, yes! I referred a salesperson to one of my friends a few years ago and he hounded her for weeks. It left a bad taste in my mouth. Do you know what I mean?

SP: You bet I do. I don't blame you for being a bit gunshy. A couple of things. . . . You may recall that it was through a referral that I came to know you.

CU: I guess you're right.

SP: Maybe it will help if I tell you how I would contact anyone you recommended to me. Would you indulge me for a minute?

CU: Sure, go ahead.

SP: Thanks. First, once you give me the name of a friend or colleague, I'll ask you to call him first. Not as a favor to me, but I suspect he would appreciate hearing from you, someone he knows, before he hears from me, a stranger. You can tell him that I've been helpful to you and that he just might find meeting with me interesting and probably helpful.

After you call, I'll contact him by phone to set up an appointment, much the same way I did with you. If it appears I can help him and he expresses interest in continuing the relationship, then I guess we have a match. And I'm sure he'll be grateful to you for hooking us together. If, on the other hand, he doesn't want to pursue a relationship, then I'll back off instantly. I promise you that I will not be a pest, and that I will act in the same professional manner I have with you.

Does that sound reasonable?

CU: I suppose so.

SP: Then, with your permission of course, I'd like to explore whom you think might benefit from the type of work I do. Let's take a look at. . . .

(And now you narrow their focus to get names and upgrade them.)

Internal Obstacles

There are many internal obstacles any salesperson may encounter. You might be afraid of jeopardizing the sale, future sales, or the relationship; you might feel you haven't served the prospect or customer enough (so, you don't deserve to ask yet); or you don't know how to ask.

It usually boils down to fear. Fear of rejection, or the fear that asking for referrals will some how damage the relationship you have with your satisfied customer.

Like most fears, this one is a ghost. In fact, it's really a projection onto your potential referral source. It's a trick your unconscious plays on you. Since you're feeling awkward about asking for the referrals, you think the other person will feel awkward being asked.

However, if you've done your best to be sincere, if you've served them well, and you've established a relationship of mutual trust, then your customers and referral alliances will not mind your request. In fact, they may be extremely happy to help you. Remember to foreshadow your request for referrals; then it will be much easier for you to ask.

Doing a good job for others, as opposed to just trying to make the sale, builds the confidence necessary to get referrals. As I've said before (and will probably say again), building a business from referrals takes a true attitude of service.

When to ask is partly an intuitive thing. When you're not asking, just make sure in your heart that it's because the time isn't right, not because you're afraid (Wimp Junction).

Most fears are really ghosts.

Please, please, please don't let fear hold you back from this most powerful way to build your career.

Keep asking for referrals

Don't forget to go back to your customers every so often for more referrals. Take them to lunch once a year, perhaps on the anniversary of when you started doing business together. Just as you keep track of your conversations with prospects and customers about other issues, you should keep track of when you asked for referrals, what the response was, and the names you collected.

When you are building your business from referrals, your relationship with customers must never end, because they are always meeting new people. Even long after you've served them, they can be referral alliances. So, keep in touch, and keep serving them in small ways.

The Referral Prospecting System

10 Important Steps

1. Serve your customers, referral alliances, and prospects well. Exceed their expectations.

2. Nurture relationships of trust and open communication.

3. Plant referral seeds constantly.

4. Ask for referrals.

5. Treat the asking with reverence and ask for their help.

6. Gain permission to explore, and narrow their focus.

7. Upgrade the referrals.

8. Warm up the prospects.

9. Update and thank your referral sources.

10. Keep asking for referrals from satisfied customers.

CHAPTER 18

Create a Referral Mindset

Referral selling is not just a bunch of techniques; it's a way to build a business and a successful sales career. The techniques merely support your mindset of building your business in this manner.

You can look at it from at least three angles:

1. You serve people well, and occasionally they provide you with referrals. Somewhat effective, but not proactive enough for me.

2. You ask for referrals when you think about it, when it "feels right" to ask. More effective, but still not proactive enough for me.

3. You create a mindset that says, "I work from referrals. I am going to achieve sustained success by serving people so well that when I ask for referrals, they are happy to give them to me." This is how I've built my business, and it's how you can build yours.

To get truly good at prospecting for referrals, you have to make it a constant habit, not just do it when you think about it. Constantly plant seeds, constantly foreshadow, constantly ask and upgrade, and constantly *give* referrals. The more you give upgraded referrals to others, the more it will be your habit to gather them.

You also want to be creative in how you go after referrals. For instance, George Jacob, a sales representative with the American Trade Bindery, uses referrals to make his sales trips more productive. "I was planning a trip to see a prospect in Dallas and wanted to maximize the value of the trip. I called two of my major accounts to see who they knew in Dallas. They gave me more names than I could schedule in one trip."

> **To get truly good at prospecting for referrals, you have to make it a constant habit, not just do it when you think about it.**

Every time you *don't* ask a customer or prospect with whom you have established good rapport and whom you have begun to serve, as you're walking out the door, think, "I just wimped out and passed up the opportunity that could take my career to a whole new level." Or better yet, as you hit Wimp Junction, think, "I wonder who they know who can lead me to the biggest sale I've ever made in my life." Then move through Wimp Junction and ask for referrals.

Here's How It's Supposed to Work

This story illustrates how building your business from referrals can become a way of life.

I had delivered a series of workshops for a small association in Baltimore. Attending the workshop was a sales rep whose name also happened to be Bill. I enjoyed having Bill M. in my program, but when it was over we went our separate ways.

About six months later, I received a phone call from the owner of Bill's company. Based on a strong referral from Bill, she wanted me to deliver some customized programs for her staff. Of course I agreed. The workshops went very well.

A few months after the programs ended, Bill moved to another company. It seemed this second company was looking to bring in an outside voice to help increase sales. This time, since Bill was so new to this company, he was reluctant to get very proactive in the process. I respected his wishes for me not to call his boss (yet), so I just mailed information.

After a couple of weeks I grew impatient. I didn't want to lose this potential sale. So, I called Bill and told him I'd like to be more proactive. He said that would be fine.

I called his boss and scheduled an appointment. A few days later I was awarded a nice contract for an ongoing program.

After I got the business, I asked the owner why he had hired me. He said that it was on the strength of Bill's referral, as well as a few references he checked into.

Had I not become more proactive in the process, I probably would not have made the sale. It was a great lesson for me—and for Bill, I might add. He has adopted my referral selling system, and it has brought him much success at his new company. I can't wait to see where Bill moves to next.

There's more to the story. Jerry H. is the company president. He is very active in his industry's association. In fact, when I met him he was about two years away from becoming chairman of the board of the national association. Jerry was an industry influencer. I wanted to serve him especially well, because I knew he could become a powerful referral alliance for me. Jerry has already written me a terrific testimonial letter. And I want to tell you of an unusual referral I got from him.

I'm just learning the game of golf. Jerry is an avid golfer, so when I told him of my newfound interest, he suggested I contact Brian or Jay at The Jay Perkins Golf Shop in Baltimore for my first set of clubs. He said he'd call ahead to make sure I got treated just right.

I said, "Thank you; I'll let you know when I'm ready." But I was thinking, "Why do I want to drive all the way from Washington, DC, to Baltimore just for a set of starter clubs?" Then I thought, "Jerry knows what he's talking about, and perhaps it will help my relationship with him grow."

I don't know all the details of what Jerry said to Brian and Jay, but when I got there to pick out some clubs, not only did I get the royal treatment, but also they were very interested in my sales seminars. A few weeks later, after they sold me a set of clubs, I sold them four sales seminars, mostly on the power of Jerry's referral.

This is how referral selling is supposed to work. One relationship leads you to another. If you serve each other well along the way, everyone wins over and over again!

Be a Referral Giver

Since building a referral business is not just a set of techniques but a mindset, you must become an expert at giving referrals. Serve your referral alliances, your customers, and your friends as best you can by *helping them with referrals* as often as you can—not just by finding prospects for them, but by helping them meet people and businesses that will serve them, whatever their need. There is no better way to send the message (or should I say plant the seed) that you work from referrals than to practice the giving side of it.

Let's say you meet someone at a business event who might become a good referral alliance. The next time you get together, do whatever you can to serve him. Try to find a way to refer him to either a prospect or someone with a product or service that will help him solve a problem.

Give referrals from your catalog

We talked much earlier about having your own "personal catalog" of products and services. It's important that you develop two types of catalogs. One is a network of companies and individuals with services related to your product or service. When you learn that prospects and customers have a need you can't fill or a problem you can't solve, you're ready to refer them to someone who can.

The other catalog is more general: it contains companies and individuals in a broad range of categories that you can refer on occasion—car mechanic, graphic artist, dry cleaner, or specialty advertising company, for example.

Practice the golden rule of referral giving

When you give referrals to other salespeople and entrepreneurs, make sure you give them in the way that you'd like to receive them. Let's say you run into someone who might be a great prospect for one of your referral alliances (or even a customer). Here are a few reminders on how to pass on this referral:

1. Get permission from the new prospect to give his or her name to your referral alliance. This way your referral alliance can be proactive and not have to wait for the prospect to call her.

2. Demonstrate enthusiasm to the prospect about who will be calling them. Tell the prospect how this salesperson has served other customers.

3. Upgrade the referral as much as you can. Have plenty of information to give to your referral alliance. Make certain to represent the information accurately.

4. Don't sit on hot referrals. Pass them on as quickly as possible.

5. Don't give the same referral to more than one or two referral alliances. If you do, make sure that all parties know.

When people ask me for referrals, I do my best to accommodate them. After I give them the names and numbers, I upgrade the referrals. Then I volunteer to warm up the prospects—to say good things about the salesperson before they call. Once someone has earned my trust and respect and has served me well, I do all I can to give him or her high-quality referrals.

If you want to receive high-quality referrals, you must give high-quality referrals.

Collect and Use
Testimonial Letters

Thind-party endorsements really work! They can be a valuable tool in helping you build credibility and value in the marketplace. If you're targeting a niche market, your prospects can see this from the testimonial letters in your information packets. A former business partner of mine, Richard Lippman, calls them "testabalonial letters," but I see them more as building blocks for my castle.

It's amazing how powerful third-party endorsements really are. Of course, that's what referral selling is all about. Having it in writing is an important tool. When you say something great about yourself, it may come across as confidence, or it may sound like bragging. When someone else says it, it becomes the truth.

If you serve your customers well, a few will send you letters every now and then. I like to be more proactive in all my sales efforts, so I've learned to *ask* for the letters.

Asking for Testimonial Letters

If I know my customer is particularly pleased, I always ask for a letter. I'll say, "I really appreciate your saying that. You know, every now and then it's helpful for me to get a letter from a satisfied client. Would you be willing to find a couple of minutes to put what you just said to me in writing and send it to me on your letterhead?" I don't think I've ever had anyone refuse to write a letter for me.

However, getting them to follow through on that agreement is another issue. I've found that if I just leave it at that simple request, I get about 40 percent of the letters promised. People don't mean to break their word; they're just busy, like everyone else. So I usually keep the process going. As soon as I hang up the phone, I send them a note thanking them for their kind words and thanking them "in advance" for the letter they'll be sending. This is a subtle reminder to keep their word.

If a happy client is an industry influencer or a center of influence, I definitely want a letter from her. If I haven't received the letter within a month or so, I'll call her on the phone. The client usually brings up the letter first and apologizes for not getting to it yet. Then I say, "That's OK, I know you're really busy. Here's an idea. Would it be helpful if I put a few thoughts on paper for you? You can edit or rewrite all you like and then send it to me on your letterhead, OK?" People always agree to this. I've collected dozens of letters this way. You may feel this is a very gutsy question to ask, and perhaps it is, but I've never had anyone refuse. They usually say, "Sure, if you don't mind."

When I call, I ask them a couple of questions or I reiterate what they already said to me. Or I ask how they benefited from my service. Then I put it in letter form—*in their own words*. They look it over and tweak it as they want. Then they retype it on their letterhead and send it out to me. I get just about every one of these letters back.

I used to suggest when I first requested the letter that I write it. However, I've found that the letters customers write themselves are usually better than mine. So I resort to helping them only when it's a letter I really want and they are dragging their feet.

Using the Testimonials

Mark works for a customized manufacturing company in Philadelphia. The day after attending one of my seminars, he put these testimonial techniques to work when he got a call from a very happy customer. Not only was she pleased with Mark's service, but also she was impressed with how the production staff handled some problems that came up with her job. So, Mark asked her to write a letter—and to mention the production staff in it.

When the letter arrived, Mark shared it with the people who had produced this job. The production folks were pleased to know that the customer appreciated their hard work. They were pleased with Mark for showing them the letter. Do you think this will help Mark when he needs more favors from production? You bet it will. Do you think the production staff will take care of this customer the next time? Count on it.

When you collect testimonial letters, it's a good idea to get a few that speak about the other people who help you deliver great service. These letters will help you with both your internal relationships and your prospecting. As your prospects look through your letters, they will see some saying good things about *you* and one or two saying good things about your *team.*

Use these letters liberally. Put them in your information packets. Use them to follow up with prospects still in your pipeline. Use short excerpts from them in brochures and newsletters. Often, when I send out a testimonial letter, I highlight a sentence or paragraph I really want my prospect to read. There's a chance she may not read the letter at all. I reduce that chance by calling her attention to it. If I'm sending a full information packet out to a prospect, in the PS of my cover letter I'll call attention to "what other satisfied clients have said about my work." I'm thinking about making a rubber stamp to stamp each letter with "Another Satisfied Client."

I've consulted with several companies that take this a step further. They create special printed pieces with a photo of the happy customer's face or place of business next to his or her testimonial letter. This adds impact to the testimony, and the customers enjoy the recognition.

Use third-party endorsements. They work!

I know of one salesperson who, after he requests a letter, faxes a simple set of guidelines. He says it helps him get the type of letter he really wants.

It is important that you make a habit of collecting testimonial letters. Use them every time you give or mail promotional literature to prospects. Sometimes I just send a couple of testimonial letters instead of my fancy brochure and the whole promotional kit. (I keep track of everything I send to my prospects and customers, including which testimonial letters have gone to whom.)

Dubin buys reams of different rag-content paper in various *business* colors (nothing too bright). He copies the testimonial letters onto this higher-quality paper. These letters will certainly stand out and get read more than letters on plain white paper. I've just started doing this myself, and it makes my promotional kit look much more polished.

Things to Include in a Testimonial Letter

Burt Dubin, in an article he wrote for Managers magazine, gave the following seven vital elements of the sure-fire recommendation letter. Try to get as many of these elements into your letter from your satisfied customer as you can.

1. The nature of the problem or challenge your referrer faced before you came along.

2. Your professional and effective presentation of options.

3. How happy your referrer is to be your client.

4. How easy and pleasant it is to work with you.

5. Any present plans for further or ongoing use of your service or products.

6. The high value, appropriateness, and importance of your insights at the first meeting.

7. Your ongoing concern for and servicing of your clients' needs.

SECTION 5

The Fourth Cornerstone

Target Niche Markets

Your Most Powerful Marketing Strategy

Targeting niche markets is the fourth and final cornerstone in building a referral business. Whether you are a small business owner or a salesperson employed by a company, niche marketing will help you substantially increase your income and put the fun back into selling. Let's start out with a definition. To me, targeting niche markets means: Positioning yourself as an expert in a target industry as it relates to your product or service and leveraging that expertise and reputation with appropriate marketing techniques so that people in the target industry will think of you first and call you. You may already be targeting some industries, or may have thought about targeting, yet you didn't really know how to make it work efficiently. Harvey Mackay calls it "niche picking."

What's the difference between marketing and selling? Basically, marketing is all the activity that makes the sale possible. Marketing makes people aware of your product or service and puts them in a position to meet you so that the sale becomes possible. Bill Brooks, author and speaker, says, "Marketing strategy is what gets you to the customer's door in the best possible light. Sales strategy is what you do when you are inside."

In *Relationship Selling,* Jim Cathcart provides an "equation of marketing, sales, and service toward achieving success." He says that marketing is generating a desire for your product or service; selling is converting that desire into transactions. Service is converting those transactions into satisfied customers. Cathcart says great marketing plus poor sales equals poverty. Great sales plus poor marketing equals burnout. Companies that are sales-activity driven usually have a certain amount of success, but without an effective marketing component, the sales reps usually end up burning out (which leads to high turnover in your sales force).

The Benefits of Targeting Niche Markets

So, marketing is a very important component in driving your referral business. Niche marketing takes the basic principles of marketing and reduces them to the level of the salesperson so that you can begin to operate as an entrepreneur within your company. If you are the owner of a small company, you too can use niche marketing strategies for incredible results.

There are at least three compelling reasons for targeting niche markets.

1. It creates word-of-mouth. A great reputation, with people saying good things about you behind your back, is the most effective way to ensure sustained success. Witness a new movie hitting the theaters. If the movie isn't any good, word-of-mouth kills it. If the movie is good, word-of-mouth takes it to new heights. Word-of-mouth often has much more impact in the marketplace than reviewers do. It's the same with books, audiotapes, and virtually anything else anyone tries to market. If the product or service is good, and enough people know about it, they start to talk about it. That's what we want for you—and it's all within your control.

2. It makes referrals easier to obtain. People within industries and affinity groups usually have many

friends and colleagues to whom they can refer you.
When they know you are concentrating your efforts
in their industry, they are usually more willing to
help you extend your influence. In my own niche
marketing efforts, I have rarely met a client who was
concerned about my calling on the competition. In
fact, quite often they are on very friendly terms. I've
received some of my best referrals to my clients'
direct competitors.

3. If you have to make any prospecting cold calls, they
   are usually much warmer to begin with, or they are
   warmed up much more quickly because people have
   heard of you. Targeting a niche market is an important part of building a referral business because it is
   so much easier to create word-of-mouth and referrals
   within a niche where people interact with each other.
   You can spread the word within a specific industry
   much more efficiently than across industries. It's
   easier to build relationships and provide value all
   along the way.

C. Richard Weylman, CSP, professional speaker and
author of *Opening Closed Doors: Keys to Reaching Hard-to-
Reach People* (Irwin Professional Publishing, 1994), gives this
example. "IBM historically assigned its sales representatives
to geographic areas. Its 62 geographic areas were defined
clearly, and a myriad of demographic and psychographic
information was available for each of these areas. However,
faced with customer demands that it try to do a better job of
relating to, and solving problems, for them, IBM has rede-
fined its markets and restructured its sales force. It now is
selling to specific industries, not geographic areas or demographic profiles."

"No matter how you have segmented your market in
the past, it is ultimately your responsibility to adjust the way
you see and define the marketplace now.

"To demystify the process, look at how people interact
and build mutually rewarding relationships with one another. You will realize quickly that they usually organize or asso-

ciate with one another based on what they do for a living, or what they do for recreation. Many also organize and associate based on their social, charitable, cultural or community interests and ethnic backgrounds.

"Remember the truism 'Birds of a feather flock together.' People associate and communicate with other people like themselves. For instance, people in the same type of business or profession join together in an association. To gain access to the marketplace, we should then divide it based on what our prospects do for a living, for recreation or where they have special interests. The advantage is that by segmenting your marketing into niches in this way, you can reach out to prospects that associate and communicate with each other. This means you can find and associate with them. They, in turn, can find and associate and communicate with you. Without these two factors, your marketing and prospecting efforts will continue to be frustrating and expensive."

> "By segmenting your marketing into niches, you can reach out to prospects that associate and communicate with each other."

I have a friend who is a sales rep for an advertising agency. She says that working these principles of niche marketing is like trying to move into a new lane while waiting at a traffic light. If you begin to inch over, trying to squeeze your car into the small space between neighboring vehicles, you may not get in. However, if you just catch the eye of the driver of the car you wish to cut in front of, he or she will almost always wave you in. Establish some recognition, and you'll be let in. The same is true in sales. If people have heard of you, even if they're not sure where, you can get past the gate-keeper and your voice-mail messages get returned. A widespread reputation overcomes barriers.

People Buy What's Familiar

Maybe you've heard the old story of the young man who joined the military and was stationed overseas for a year. Before he left, he bought 365 postcards. He mailed one to his girlfriend every day. For about 10 months, she wrote back regularly. Then her letters stopped. When the young man returned home, he found his girlfriend married to the mailman. People buy what's familiar, as Rick Hill says.

Niche marketing in a specific industry or affinity group will create that familiarity for you. Most of the referrals I have obtained over the years have been to my clients' competitors or others within the same industry. When your customers know that you are niche marketing in their industry and that you work from referrals, they become more willing to refer you to people they know.

When you target a niche market, your perceived expertise in that industry adds value to the transaction. That added value to the transaction will often keep the sale from coming down to price. Earlier I mentioned that prospects who like and trust you will give you referrals. Well, when you target an industry and bring that added value to the first appointment, you speed up the whole process. Your industry expertise may help you serve your prospects right on the spot. Once served, they are more likely to serve you. Don't forget to plant the seed that you work from referrals. Put these two together, and you'll walk away with referrals from your very first appointments.

The Potential Disadvantage to Targeting Niche Markets

There is one disadvantage to targeting niche markets of which you must beware. Unless you have been hired specifically to target an industry or you have created your business to target a specific industry, I don't recommend putting all your eggs in one basket. Instead, keep a broad base of selling activity. If you focus exclusively on one industry and it goes through a downturn or other problems, you may not be able to recover. But if you have a broader base, you can absorb your target industry's difficulties.

If you are brand new to selling or have just started a sales job with a new company, move slowly with these strategies, because targeting niche markets requires a certain amount of activity that does not bring in immediate business. Although over time it will bring you increased business, initially it will take you away from the all-important selling activities such as being on the phone or being face to face with customers or potential customers. As a new salesperson, or an experienced salesperson new to your company, you need to bring in business any way you can. You need to bring in sales from as many quarters as possible, and I don't want you to restrict yourself. Use all the other ideas presented in this book to build your referral business, and the niche marketing strategies will fall into place.

If you have been in your job for a long time and you have a broad base of established business, or you have marketing programs already in place that will bring you a predictable income, *now* you are in the best position to target niche markets.

For Committed Sales Professionals Only

Whether you are new or have been selling for 20 years, niche marketing is for serious sales professionals and business owners only. Niche marketing requires a high level of commitment, not just to sales and your business but to working the niche marketing strategies so that you'll do what it takes to make them successful. If you work them halfway, you'll get halfway results. But if you're truly committed to working the strategies and you're truly committed to yourself as a salesperson, then you will reach new levels of success by targeting niche markets.

When you target niche markets or industries, reputation is everything. You need to go the extra mile. And you can't burn bridges, because word-of-mouth spreads faster within specific industries. Every transaction, every encounter, has to be handled with the utmost professionalism. Everyone is always a prospect, at least in the sense of helping you build your reputation. If a company is too small or doesn't really need your product or service, you still must have an attitude of service. Even people in your target industry who aren't prospects should be treated with professionalism and dignity. It takes a serious commitment to do that great a job.

CHAPTER 21

My Personal Story of Targeting

As a professional speaker and seminar leader, I have targeted the printing industry, among others. This is one reason many of the examples in this book involve printing sales. Many of my own niche marketing efforts can easily be translated to your world.

When I first started niche marketing, I did some *free* work for some companies. I did it to be immersed in their industry and to learn what their issues were so I could tailor my seminars to their needs and goals. I spoke in front of groups of salespeople and company owners for no fee to begin creating my reputation. I learned a lot about how I wanted to target this industry and adjusted both my message and my approach as I learned.

I still occasionally speak for free when I know the room will be full of prospects. This enhances my reputation and significantly warms up that next phone call to a prospect who has heard me speak. (More on this later.)

You may have a product or service that you can't give away in any way, shape, or form. But if you can, then do it! Serve people in your target industry as quickly as you can. Gain some success stories and some satisfied customers as soon as possible. You will learn so much, so quickly, and you will make adjustments in your approach to the industry.

During one of my first seminars in the printing industry, I met a salesperson who was targeting credit unions. He had sold some printing to a credit union and created a satisfied customer that kept coming back. He thought, "Well, this credit union buys this much printing; maybe there are some other credit unions that buy this much or more." So, he started to pursue other credit unions. As he got two, three, four, and five credit unions as loyal customers he became known as a credit union printer—even though his company was basically just a regular commercial printer and served many types of customers in many industries. He began to know credit unions' needs better than any other printer in town, and he brought that added value to every prospecting opportunity. He knew their problems, so he could help fix them. He saw how other credit unions were doing things, and he could bring some of that knowledge and experience to bear with new prospects.

Protecting Client Confidentiality

Let me issue a word of warning: When you work within a specific industry and you see how certain companies are solving their problems, you have to value their confidentiality. You have to be careful about what you tell their competitors. You certainly want to position yourself as knowledgeable in their industry, as someone who can help solve their problems with your product or service. And you want to use your experiences to help new prospects and customers. However, be very careful about what you reveal. I've often had clients ask me to not share certain ideas or bits of information with others in their industry. I've signed a few nondisclosure agreements. Just maintain a high sense of integrity, professionalism, and confidentiality and you'll be fine.

When I started targeting the printing industry, I met an insurance salesperson who was also targeting the printing industry. He was selling business insurance to many of the printers in the Washington, DC, area. He knew their needs better than insurance salespeople who weren't specializing in that industry. He sold beyond the printing industry, but he made the printing industry a niche market for himself—always being careful to never reveal any proprietary information.

Choosing My Niche Market

Why did I choose the printing industry? Well, I had owned a book publishing company, and I had been buying printing for 14 years. I had brokered printing (meaning I re-sold printing to others). And for about a year after selling my publishing company, I worked in sales with an electronic prepress business. So, naturally I picked an industry in which I had a significant amount of knowledge, experience, and success.

Before I made one call to a printer to try to sell my sales training and customer service training programs, I took a couple of people in the printing industry to lunch. I told them what I was planning to do and made sure I was in tune with the needs of the industry. I wanted to verify that the things *I thought* were important to them *were* important. I learned a lot. With each person I called, I got better and better in creating a conversation that interested them and that led to sales.

Most people who target an industry already know at least a few individuals in that industry.

Say you've decided to target an industry or other affinity group. Before you do anything else, meet with some of the people in that industry on an informal basis, not a selling basis. Tell them what you are planning to do and that you need their experience and wisdom to help you make a more powerful start.

Most people who target an industry already know at least a few individuals in that industry (or know someone who does). If you don't have quick access to anyone in your target industry, you may have to make a couple of those dreaded cold calls to ask for help. It's always better when they've been warmed up through referrals, but it's not necessary. Tell them right off the bat that you're not trying to sell them anything. Tell them that they have a very good reputation in their industry; you value their knowledge and you're planning on targeting their industry; and you want to make sure that you do it with maximum effectiveness.

Not everybody is going to give you the time, but some people will. All you need are two or three people to get you started, to give you an hour or two here and there, and to make sure that your approach is the right one. A by-product of these informational meetings is that you have started a relationship with people who can become prospects down the road. Many of the people who helped educate me became prospects and referral alliances later on, and some have become clients. I waited several months before coming back to them in a selling mode. And I was honest with them: I told them I had taken their advice, and now I had some great stuff that might be perfect for them. Getting the sales appointment was easy.

Positioning Myself

Next I got on the phone and started calling printers to gain sales appointments. I used my *buyer's* perspective to distinguish myself from all the other sales trainers in the market. Wouldn't their salespeople and their customer service people like to know what a buyer thinks? What did it take to win my business and loyalty? That angle (position) went a long way in getting me started.

I told people that I was specializing in their industry. This helped because they wanted someone who knew their business and the issues their people faced.

I also used my experience in their industry to differentiate myself from a lot of my competition. Many people do sales and customer service programs, and I wasn't the only one calling on these people in the printing industry. However, I was one of the few *targeting* the printing industry. By virtue of my work with trade associations, the associations began referring me to customers, and people started calling me because they had seen my name in conjunction with association activities.

Whatever your product, whatever your service, people will recognize the added value your targeting brings to them and will want to deal with you because of that added value. Even if their issues aren't really much different from the issues in other industries, it's their perception that counts.

> **People will recognize the added value your targeting brings to them.**

Position yourself as a resource, not just a vendor, to your target industry. Practice "partnering" with companies within a specific industry. Don't just be a source for your product or service; be a resource of valuable knowledge and information that keeps them turning to you over and over again. Partnering means finding out what success means to your prospects and customers and then helping them achieve it.

Other Targeting Tactics

I presented speeches and seminars to the local printing associations in Baltimore and Washington, and I joined several of them. When I spoke to these groups, I was speaking to many prospects. I asked the national association, Printing Industries of America, about its publications and conferences. After a few sessions of speaking and attending meetings, people started to know who I was. Sometimes they wouldn't even know how they had heard of me. I'd be talking to a sales manager, and he'd say, "Where have I heard your name before?" Then I'd tell him that I specialized in the industry and I was doing work with the association.

I created a special brochure for the printing industry (we'll talk a little bit more about that later). When I write a letter to someone in an industry I'm targeting, I put after my name, "Speaker and Seminar Leader for the Printing [or other target industry] Industry." That drives home the point that I am an expert in their field.

CHAPTER 22

Targeting Your Niche Market

ere are specific areas in
which you can concentrate
your efforts to make niche
marketing work for you. You don't have to act on all of these
ideas and techniques to become more successful. In fact, you
won't have the hours or the energy to undertake them all at
once. However, over time, as you see these techniques start
to yield results for you, read this book again to be reminded
of more things that you can do to generate even more referrals and sales.

Choose *Your* Niche Market or Industry

I know a stockbroker and financial planner who had planned
to become an actress. She majored in theater arts in college.
She enjoyed entertainment and broadcasting. But like many
of us, she took a different road when it came to earning a
living. This stockbroker hooked up with a local radio
station, and now she does the Wall Street reports at the end
of each day. She has found a way to use her experience and
interest in broadcasting and theater in her sales career. Being
heard on a very powerful radio station in the Washington
area has contributed significantly to her success.

I recently met a sales manager with a company in Wisconsin. He tells his salespeople to consider their interests when they pick target industries. He figures that if they like their target industry, the reps will enjoy the selling more—and then they'll sell more!

What industries have you worked in before? For what industries do you have some affinity? What industry do you find fun? Answering these questions can help you narrow your focus.

Another way to find your target market is to look at your customer base. With whom are you doing business now? Are there two, three, four, or five customers in the same industry? If so, you're already niche marketing—or at least you've got a great base. You already know what their concerns are. Now all you have to do is leverage this experience.

When you're at the beginning stages of niche marketing, don't be afraid to ask for help.

Are there any clients that you really enjoy? Maybe you have only one in a particular industry, but you really enjoy doing business with her. Why not focus on other businesses like hers?

When you're at the beginning stages of niche marketing, don't be afraid to ask for help. Talk to people with whom you have done business. More important, talk to people you don't even know if you think you might like to target their industry. You will be surprised at how much help they'll give you.

I have a friend who decided he wanted to target an industry, so he invited a lot of his personal and business friends over for dinner. (He happens to be a gourmet cook, but you can order take-out if you like.) He created a focus group, or what Napoleon Hill (author of *Think and Grow Rich*, Fawcett Crest, revised edition, 1960) called a "mastermind." Hill said that when two minds come together, a third mind is created that comes up with ideas and perspectives the two minds would not achieve separately. My friend had a mastermind group just for himself that evening. He said, "Thank you for coming over. Let's talk about *me* for a while."

He told them what he was trying to do. He wanted to pick one, two, or three industries and, over time, target those industries with his marketing and sales efforts. He asked them to help him come up with the industries that were right for him. This brainstorming session gave him all sorts of ideas and strategies, and he is successfully niche marketing in two industries, with plans for more in a couple of years.

Determine the Universe of Your Target Industry

Once you have found an industry you might want to target, you need to determine the universe of that industry. Is it big enough to make it worth niche marketing? Is it big enough within your local area, or do you have to become regional or national in your scope for the universe to be large enough? Make sure there are enough businesses within the industry, within the geographic area where you wish to do business.

Figure Out How to Reach Your Target

If this industry has a local or national association (and most industries do), get a list of the association members even it means joining the association. There are also directories in the library on various industries. Even the phone book can help. If you cannot determine who your prospects are, or if they will be hard to reach, find another industry to target.

Work the Numbers

Once you determine the universe and know that you can reach your prospects, you want to work the numbers a little bit. You want to determine the sales and profit potentials. If you have done business with one or more companies in your target industry, extrapolate from the volume of business you have done with them. You also want to look at the profitability of doing business in this industry, not just the total sales volume. Take a little time to run some numbers and make sure that it's an industry worth targeting.

Get to Know Your Competition

If you've picked a good industry to target, there's a strong chance someone else is already doing it. Don't let that deter you. If the universe is big enough, there's plenty to go around. Learn as much about your competitors as possible. Get their promotional materials. Get copies of their guarantees and service policies. Watch their ads and articles in the newspapers. If they are publicly traded, call your stockbroker and purchase one share of their stock; you'll be on the mailing list for their annual report and other valuable correspondence. Call the Better Business Bureau. Learn your competitors' strengths and weaknesses, and position yourself to be strong where they are weak. Find creative ways to get on their mailing lists.

Also, *never* talk down your competition. It's unprofessional, and it calls into question the judgment of those who have used them—like your prospects!

Form Referral Alliances with Niche Suppliers

Forge working relationships with niche suppliers with whom you don't compete head to head. Referrals from another salesperson can be very powerful. It's a great idea to form alliances with salespeople in noncompeting companies already targeting your niche. As with all referral alliances, make sure you both know how you benefit your customers. Meet for lunch or breakfast every now and then to share information.

Look for Overlaps with Your Target Industry

Attached to the printing industry I found the paper, ink, and equipment industries. I knew that as I began to target the printing industry, I could also target these related industries.

Suppose you're niche marketing in the hotel industry. The related industries might include resorts, food and beverage manufacturers, cruise lines, meetings, and entertainment, among others. Any major industry that you target has related industries that can be added to your marketing efforts.

Read What Your Target Prospects Are Reading

Virtually every industry has magazines, trade journals, and newsletters that most of your prospects read. The national and local associations publish these, as do independent companies. How do you find out what they're reading? Call the associations and ask what they publish. They may also be able to tell you about other publications. Talk to your existing customers or prospects within this target industry and ask them what industry publications they are reading.

To get a free copy of a particular publication, call the journal or magazine and ask for a current media kit. A media kit is what they send to prospective advertisers, and I think you can legitimately call yourself a prospective advertiser. Get at least one issue of each publication, more if possible.

Read each publication to learn more about your target industry. Is this publication worth subscribing to? Is it one for which you might want to write articles? (More on this later.)

Many industry magazines and trade journals will send publications to people free just to boost their circulation numbers so that they can charge more for their advertising.

Use these publications as tools for learning the industry and identifying prospects. Remember, the more you know about a prospect before you call, the more powerful your call will be.

Your local reference librarian can help you locate most of the trade journals in your target industry. You might start with Standard Rate and Data's *Business and Consumer Publications*.

How to Pick Your Market Niche

In *Opening Closed Doors*, C. Richard Weylman offers some important considerations in picking one or more target markets. Here are a few:

Consider these market profitability issues.

- Is the market growing or declining?
- Are the sales and/or incomes of this market in growth or decline?
- How can you position yourself and your company in this market?
- What opportunities are there for spin-off markets?
- Which of your competitors are currently selling these people, and how are they positioned?
- What is the potential dollar volume you can sell in this market?
- Does the market have a need for your products or services?
- Could you repackage your products or services to fit the needs of this market?

Consider these market accessibility issues.

- What is their common culture: ethnic, business, recreation, or interest?
- How do they associate with each other—through associations, clubs, or special-interest organizations?
- Do they have newsletters, trade magazines, bulletins, or other means of targeted communication with their colleagues?
- Do these people have a word-of-mouth network and refer suppliers to one another?
- Are there targeted lead sources available for this niche?
- How often do the people in this niche meet with one another, professionally or socially?
- Do you feel an affinity, link, or connection to the people in this market?

Cultivating Your Niche

Once you've determined one or more niche markets to target and learned a bit about them, it's time to start cultivating your niche. Here are assorted ideas and strategies that will help you create and leverage your reputation. I've used every one of them at one time or another.

Get Involved in Trade Associations

There are national associations, state associations, and local associations. Any decent library has books or lists of associations, usually in the reference section. *The Encyclopedia of Associations* not only lists all the associations and all the information about them, but also indexes them in various ways, including key words, industry, and geographic location. Some industries have more than one association serving them.

The reference books will tell you how many members the associations have. (That's not the number of businesses in that industry; it's just the number of businesses that have chosen to join that particular association.) The books will often tell you how many conventions or conferences they have. Under the national association listing, often they'll tell you how many regional, state, and local associations there are. If you don't know how to get in touch with your local association, ask the national association.

Don't rush out and join the association right away. You can usually attend a meeting as a guest before you actually have to join. I joined several associations prematurely and spent money that I didn't really need to spend. Try a meeting or two as a guest. Once you are sure about this target industry, then it's time to join the association.

Use the association to enhance your visibility. Weylman calls it "promotion through participation."

As a member, you will have access to some products and services that can be very helpful in your niche marketing efforts, such as a membership list and regular publications. After you join, be sure to get a list of all the benefits, so you don't miss out on any.

A few years ago, I delivered a full-day customer service workshop for a printing industry association in metropolitan Washington. The association promoted this training for some time, so my name was out in front of lots of prospects. One printing company didn't feel it could afford to send all its sales reps to the training, because they would be away from the business for a full day during the week. So, the company called the association and said, "Would Bill Cates be available to come in on a weekend?" The association contact worked like an agent for me. Just by virtue of my working with the association, people see that I'm knowledgeable in their industry, and they call me. I couldn't ask for a better selling situation. And you can create the same situation for yourself.

Use the association to enhance your visibility. Weylman calls it "promotion through participation." The more you become truly active, the more relationships you can forge.

I know one very successful financial advisor, Alex, who recently headed up his target industry's charity event of the year. This brought him great visibility over an entire year. And he worked with many centers of influence within his niche and from other parts of the business community. He told me that he can trace six new clients directly from this activity, and he feels these six clients will lead him to many others. It's just a matter of time, planting seeds, and asking!

Identify the Industry Influencers

One of the most powerful things you can do to create a reputation in a target industry is to identify and serve the industry influencers. You may start with the local influencers and eventually move to the national level. The industry influencers in your target industry are the presidents of the associations, members of boards, people who have had significant success, and others who are just very active in one way or another. Find ways to get to know and serve these people as soon as you can. And serve them well, because they can make or break you.

Serving these people can mean making them satisfied customers. Or it can mean helping them develop association projects and plan charity events. Since most of these people are very successful, they already know that the secret to success is "meeting people through other people." Heavy seed-planting is called for. Make sure they know that you're niche marketing in their industry and that you could use their help in expanding your business.

Many industries have a "Who's Who" type of directory, which your library may have. Weylman suggests you create a "Ten Most Wanted" list. By doing some research and asking other influencers, you can easily identify 10 (or more) people who should know about you and whom you should serve quickly.

Write Articles for Industry Publications

Write articles that relate to your product or service as it is used by your target industry. A printing salesperson could write an article on how to find the right printer, or how to better understand the new digital technology. Someone who sells financial services could write articles that teach people about the latest investment options. Come up with some themes based on teaching your target industry how to better utilize your type of service. Make sure the articles have lots of practical knowledge. Checklists, quizzes, and the like are always popular.

This article must *not* be one long advertisement for you or your company. It must be full of usable information. The purpose is not to sell; it is to establish yourself in that industry. Trade journals usually won't run a piece that's too self-promotional, and even if they do, readers will not appreciate it.

Many good things can happen when you have articles published in industry publications. You get the opportunity to show yourself as an expert in that industry. You can make reprints of the article, adding the banner from the front of the publication. When you send out information to prospects, you can use the reprint to demonstrate that you specialize in their industry. Send the reprints to current customers in your target industry as another way to stay in touch. Use them to follow up with prospects.

Exposure in industry journals and magazines is a great way to get you past the gatekeeper or through the voice-mail barrier, because people start to know who you are.

Produce a Company Newsletter

If you don't already put out a regular newsletter, it may be time for you to get serious about this great communication device.

Of course, the most effective newsletter you could produce would be exclusively for your target industry. I've published two almost identical newsletters. One was my generic publication and one was my target newsletter. They contained all the same basic information, but the target newsletter reflected the target industry in its banner and in some of the articles. If you do put out a generic newsletter, make sure that everything in it is in some way relevant to your target industry.

Special Reports or Booklets

Now that we have moved from the Industrial Age to the Information Age, there is no better way to create a reputation as an expert in a target industry than to provide information to your prospects and customers. Many salespeople who target industries create small information booklets or "special reports." A 16- to 32-page publication can relate your product or service to your prospects' and customers' industry and buying situation. While this publication has information about your product/service, it is not a promotional piece. It is an educational piece. As you educate your prospects, they begin to see you as *the* expert and they see your product/service in a whole new light.

In most cases you should give this report away for free; but always put a price tag on it to increase the perceived value. A general report might be titled "How to Buy Printing," "How to Buy Your Next Computer," "How to Select a Real Estate Agent to Help You Sell Your Home," "How to Buy Financial Services," or "How to Buy Hotel Meeting Services." A more specific, timely report might be called "How the New Round of Tax Laws Affects Your Investment Strategy," or "How to Purchase Printing in This Digital World." You get the idea.

This report can be a great icebreaker for new contacts, a follow-up item to keep the selling "courtship" alive, a thank-you for new customers, and/or a way to stay in touch with existing customers. It will be most powerful if it is targeted to one specific industry and says so on the cover. (For example, "What Hotels Should Look for in Their Next Computer Upgrade.") A generic publication can still be effective, but it must be written in such a way that it is all relevant to your target industry.

Use Media Publicity

Did you know that anywhere from 50 to 80 percent of the stories in your newspaper were placed through press releases and other publicity efforts? You may not want to believe this, but I can tell you it's true. Beyond the front-page news, most of the stories that appear in newspapers and in magazines do so because there's someone out there pushing that topic, issue, or newsworthy event to the press. Someone persuades an editor that the information is of interest to readers, and an article is born.

The key to getting an article placed or getting an event covered is to make sure that it's newsworthy. It must contain information that will benefit readers, whether some new knowledge or a new perspective.

Taking a strong, even controversial, stand on an issue will get media and reader attention. If what you have to say is powerful and helpful, you stand a chance of being published. As soon as I finish writing this book, I plan to write a series of articles designed to help me publicize it. My first article is already started and my working title is, "It's Time to Put Cold Calling on Ice." I will talk about how cold calling is a dying sales strategy. This is somewhat controversial, because some people are still having some success with cold calling. But that success will diminish quickly as people get harder to reach by phone and become even less receptive to cold calls.

> **Taking a strong, even controversial, stand on an issue will get media and reader attention.**

Rarely does a large newspaper or magazine print a press release word for word, but quite a few of the smaller publications do. I've had many press releases printed exactly as I wrote them. People say, "Bill, that was a great article I saw about you in such-and-such publication." And I say, "Yeah, it was, thanks." And I wrote it. It was my press release!

Create releases that are newsworthy. Let's say you sell insurance, and you're niche marketing in the hotel industry. Making a large sale to a well-known company is a newsworthy event. Just make sure you get permission from your new customer to publicize the sale. Or, every time your company comes out with a new product or service that will benefit your target industry, you can write a press release designed to make it look as if the product or service were created just for that industry.

Remember the fundamental selling principle: Talk about your features in terms of benefits. When you mention a new product, new location, or any other feature of your company worth writing about in a press release, always put it in terms of the benefits to your customers. "XYZ Company Has Moved to a New Location—To Serve Customers Better."

All you need to do is contact the magazine, journal, or newsletter and ask who should receive a press release on the topic you plan to cover. Then send it on. If you have a publicity photo (which you should), send it. Many small publications give preference to press releases and articles submitted with photos.

There are many books about the fine points of writing press releases. Consult one of these books and follow its guidelines before sending yours off. If you try to wing it, your odds of having your press release considered will go way down.

The important thing about approaching the industry press, or any press, with news releases or a story idea is that it can't appear to be self-serving. Certainly you can be quoted in the release or article, and your product or service should be mentioned, but it can't read like one long ad. It has to be newsworthy.

If your release prompts the publication to write a full article on the topic, a reporter may call some of your competitors to make it look like a fair article. That's fine; your product or service will only look better by comparison.

With this new awareness, look at some of the articles in newspapers, magazines, and particularly trade journals. Look at the headlines and the topics being discussed. What similar topics can you write about that relate to your product or service? You're not a good writer? That's all right. Just talk your thoughts into a tape recorder and transcribe them. Then find an editor. Find a friend, or a loved one, or a professional to edit your news release at a reasonable rate. You can even call your target publication for the names of some freelance editors.

Create Educational Opportunities

Many companies invite prospects and customers into their office or plant to show them the latest updates in their industry. Some companies sponsor these events in hotels around the city. Use your creativity to come up with educational opportunities for your target industry. Even if you are not in the training business, can you go in-house and conduct some training programs, maybe teaching them how to use your product or service better? Host a luncheon. Sponsor other speakers.

These events cannot be ads for you and your company. You really must deliver the information.

Educational events will serve at least two purposes. First, they will establish you and your company as the experts in your field—especially as it relates to your target industry. Second, they'll give you another "warm" way to meet with prospects and customers. Invite your current customers to bring their industry colleagues to these events. Now you can be introduced to a prospect by a satisfied customer.

Sponsor an Event

Your target industry is probably full of opportunities for you to gain widespread recognition through sponsorship. Perhaps your target industry has awards ceremonies and the awards are sponsored in some way. Perhaps your target industry, particularly on a local level, sponsors certain charities. Find out what industry events go on and find ways to attach your name to those events. Make the sponsorship directly from you, not just your company. Instead of the brochure saying, "This award is being sponsored by XYZ Company," have it say, "This award is being sponsored by John Doe of XYZ Company."

If you sponsor a hospitality suite at a trade show, a cocktail party at a convention, or a similar event, have it come from you (as well as your company).

Master Public Speaking

When you target a specific industry or affinity group, speaking in front of groups within your niche can be very powerful. There is no better way to attract new customers than by demonstrating your expertise in a speech. Refer to Appendix A for more information on this powerful sales tool.

Adjust the Way You Do Business

Every industry has its own style of doing business. Some industries work with net 30 terms, some with net 10, some with no terms at all. Study your target industry to see how it buys your product or service and other products and services. Be prepared to adjust to the prevailing practices. If you've been selling your product/service to other industries in one manner, you can't assume that this new industry will do business with you in the same way.

Examine your various terms and policies such as invoicing, pricing, and delivery, as well as the terminology you use. For example, when I sold my books to gift stores and other non-bookstore outlets, I gave net 30 terms, with no returns (except if damaged or defective). But when I sold to bookstores, I had to allow returns, because that's the way that industry does business. If I didn't allow returns, they wouldn't do business with me, simple as that.

In trying to determine how you position your product or service for your target industry, ask: What are your competitors doing? How are they pricing their product or service? What terms are they giving? Should you offer the same terms because that's what the industry expects, or could you give yourself an edge by offering slightly better terms?

See if you can answer the question my friend, marketing expert Fred Berns, likes to ask, "What is your *only...*?" What is it about your product or service that's different from anybody else's, particularly in how it may relate to your target industry? The answer should be a significant part of how you position yourself in your target market.

Adapt Your Marketing Materials

A brochure or other promotional piece will always be more effective if it's tailored to your target industry. It builds so much more value in doing business with you. To which company and salesperson would you give extra consideration, one with a generic product/service or one with an offering that's tailored to *your* industry?

When I created my brochure for my sales and customer service programs, I created a variation that was identical except for certain words throughout the brochure that related it to the printing industry. Now I have two brochures, one that's generic and one that's related to the printing industry. Create the two versions and ask the printer to change the black plate during the printing run. It won't cost you much more, and it will be worth it!

Place Ads Your Prospects Will See

Once again, remember Rick Hill's slogan: "People buy what's familiar." Given the choice between some person or product they've heard of before and one that's unknown to them, they'll go with what's familiar. If you don't believe this, next time you're in the grocery store, watch yourself make buying decisions. We all buy what's familiar. That's why advertising works.

And advertising does work, depending on what you want it to do. Once you have progressed in your niche marketing activities, perhaps six months to a year down the road, consider well-placed, targeted advertising. I say "consider" because I've seen so many salespeople and so many companies waste money on advertising. Advertising generally does not bring sales. Unless you have a very specific offer, it generally doesn't prompt people to call you. Advertising creates an impression, and sometimes those impressions are very valuable if you are trying to present yourself as an expert in the industry. Your ads in the industry publications create familiarity.

Your ads in the industry publications create familiarity.

For instance, your local industry association may publish a newsletter that includes people's business card ads, or similar small ads. This can have some value. It is an economical way to create familiarity. When you do reach prospects, they will have heard of you (from somewhere) and they will associate you with their industry.

If you do advertise, be very careful where you place it. Start slowly. To find out if your ads are actually bringing in prospects directly, code them. (You can always ask, but often people don't remember.)

There are many ways to code your ads. You can tell the readers to ask for some fictitious person. When the prospect calls, you can say, "Jane Doe isn't in at the moment. May I help you?" Or you can use variations on your name in the ad. I might use William Cates, or Will Cates, or Mr. Cates. When people ask for "William," I know which ad prompted the phone call.

You can also code your ads with department numbers or offer numbers. No matter how you choose to code your ad, it's a good idea to do it. You'll be better able to track the results of your ad campaign.

In his book *Beware the Naked Man Who Offers You His Shirt*, Harvey Mackay offers two important rules to follow when placing advertising. He says, "Don't be your own copywriter." If you're going to the expense of placing advertising, hire a professional to write the copy for you. If you don't, you're throwing your money out the window.

Mackay also says, "Don't play it safe." Make sure your ad stands out, both graphically and verbally, in whatever publication you select. Design a creative offer that will attract attention. Use color if you can afford it.

Create a Reputation with Direct Mail

Staying with the theme "People buy what's familiar," consider using direct mail to target your industry. I use the word "consider" again because I have seen so many salespeople in so many companies waste so much money on direct mail. They think these beautiful mailing pieces are going to bring in business, but they just don't. They do create positive impressions—for the people who *open* the mail. But they don't always get to your target prospect. Direct mail can have a place as part of your familiarity mix. In fact, it can play a powerful role. The key is repetition. If you have the choice of mailing to 6,000 people once or 2,000 people three times, go with the latter. The more they see from you, the more they are likely to actually read what you send.

When you decide to implement a direct mail strategy, budget for at least three pieces to each person on your list. Better yet, make the program ongoing—anywhere from four to 12 mailings per year.

In my niche marketing workshops, the question often comes up, "Should I send it bulk mail or first class?" For bulk mail you need at least 200 items, so if you're mailing fewer than 200, it goes first class. I'm inclined to mail first class up to 500 pieces. With first class, you'll get more delivered, and what can't be delivered comes back to you with a change of address (which is important for your list maintenance). Plus, a first-class mailing is more like regular business correspondence. If it's under an ounce or under, it's very economical to mail first class.

If it's over an ounce, the cost may become prohibitive. The up side of bulk rate is that it's cheaper; the down side is that it takes longer to deliver and it takes longer to prepare. To get the bulk-mail rate, you have to presort the mail by zip code.

It's not that complicated. In fact it's pretty easy to learn, and you can even hire someone inexpensive (such as a student) to do most of it for you. Or you can send it out to a mailing service with reasonable rates. If you are going with bulk mail, consider using bulk-mail stamps. It takes longer because the stamps have to be affixed (as opposed to having your bulk-rate permit printed on the envelope), but they make it look more like first class.

There are many books on how to use direct mail effectively. I recommend that you get the advice of those experts. If you want to create a reputation in a target industry, begin a simple mailing program. Keep it simple, because if it isn't, you probably won't keep it going. If you don't keep it going, you'll just be spending your money, not *investing* it!

Harness the Power of Testimonial Letters

Even if you aren't yet niche marketing an industry, you should be collecting testimonial letters. These third-party endorsements can be enormously helpful in establishing your credibility and value. These letters become part of your information packet and can help show prospects that you've targeted their industry. Refer back to Chapter 19 for details on how to collect testimonials most effectively.

Use Industry Publications to Stay in Touch

Read the trade journals and clip the articles that support your activities or the activities of your prospects or customers. Let's say that you sell computers, and there is an article in a trade journal that talks about computers. Maybe it gives pointers for choosing the right computer. Make copies of that article and send it out to your prospects and your customers. It's another way to stay in touch, and it reinforces the fact that you are an expert in *their* industry.

The articles you clip and send may have nothing to do with what you sell. They may interest just the individual prospect or customer. When you send customers things that have nothing to do with what you sell, it's even more powerful. They see that you are looking out for their success in an unselfish way. This builds trust.

Modify Existing Products/Services or Create New Ones

As you begin to learn the needs of your target industry, you can look for ways to modify products and services or even create new ones that are tailored specifically to the industry. Here's a way I made this work for me.

A woman who owned a pick-your-own strawberry farm published a strawberry cookbook and sold it at her farm. She also sold it to a small association of pick-your-own strawberry farms. Through this modest distribution network she sold close to 400 books annually. She considered this successful.

She brought me in to help her upgrade the product. She wanted me to help her create a better cover and text, and to help with the marketing. Unfortunately, that relationship turned sour. She basically took my ideas and never paid me for them; it was not a good situation. But from that mini-disaster came a great opportunity—a jackpot.

I started to think about how I could put together a strawberry cookbook and could probably do a better job than she. I could market it more effectively, and there are probably more pick-your-own farms than the 200 in her association. So, I went to an author who had already written a cookbook for me and asked, "Could you put together a small book on cooking with strawberries?" She said, "Certainly." I had photographed a bowl of strawberries many years before. I had a print of this photo hanging in my kitchen. Now I could really put that photo to use as the book's cover.

I called the department of agriculture in every state and asked if they had a listing of pick-your-own strawberry farms in their state. Almost every state that had any strawberry industry at all sent me a list. I put them on my computer, and in a few weeks I had 1,500 addresses.

I put together a simple but professional-looking direct-mail piece and mailed it to these strawberry farms a couple of months before strawberry season started. The first year, I sold 10,000 strawberry cookbooks! The second year, I sold 15,000. Over the eight years that I had my publishing company, I sold well over 100,000 strawberry cookbooks. Talk about turning a lemon into lemonade—or should I say strawberry jam?

Now, that's niche marketing an industry, isn't it? And there's more. After the first year or so, I thought, what else could I sell to pick-your-own farm operations? What else do they sell? Well, a lot of them also grow apples. So I called the state departments of agriculture again and got the addresses of 1,600 pick-your-own apple farms around the country.

I produced an apple cookbook called *Apple Magic*. I put together another direct-mail piece and sent it out to these farms. The first year, I sold about 8,000 copies. The second year, I sold 20,000 copies. It turned out that the apple industry was even larger than the pick-your-own strawberry industry, and the selling season was longer. The strawberry season in any one place is only about three weeks and they can sell only so many books in three weeks. In the seven years that I had that title on the market, I sold well over 150,000 copies.

The more you learn about your target industry, the more creative you can become with products and services just for it.

I learned through selling the apple book that apple growers need honeybees to pollinate the apple blossoms. Therefore, most apple growers have apiaries. That's why at most country produce stands that sell apples you'll also find jars of local honey.

So, I produced a honey cookbook. It did not sell as well as the strawberry and the apple books, but it sold 4,000 to 6,000 copies a year, just to that target market. I also sold all three cookbooks to more generic markets such as cooking stores, gourmet stores, and grocery stores, which bought thousands of copies.

In addition, I found out that a lot of the apple farms and strawberry farms also sold other produce, either pick-your-own or already picked. I came up with a vegetable cookbook that I sold to these target markets and to my generic markets as well. I sold literally thousands and thousands of copies every year.

The more you learn about your target industry, the more creative you can become with products and services just for it.

Who Do You Know Who Practices Niche Marketing?

Now that you know a little bit more what *niche marketing* is all about, stop and think. Do you know any salespeople now who are targeting specific industries? Do you know any salespeople within your organization, or in other organizations, who are practicing niche marketing as just described? If you do, I suggest that you make an appointment to have lunch or dinner with them—to learn from them.

CHAPTER 24

Your Targeting Plan

If you want niche marketing to work for you, you need to create a plan and then work the plan. (A trite phrase, but oh so true!) First, identify the ideas in this book that you are likely to do right away. That becomes your short-term plan. Then identify the things that you're going to do down the road, when you have a little more time or you have had a little success. This becomes part of your mid-range plan. Create a time line and put reminders in your calendar to keep things moving.

It should go without saying (but I'll say it anyway) that this plan needs to be flexible. As you learn more about what you're doing, you're going to change and adapt. I heard an expression that fits perfectly: "Well begun is half done." When you begin with a sturdy plan that allows flexibility, you are halfway to your goal.

Another key element in getting niche marketing to work for you, particularly if you work for someone else, is to get support from others (such as your boss). That's why it's important to run the numbers. Attractive gross and net potentials will help you gain buy-in from others.

This support from above is important because you will be engaged in some activities that will not yield instant results. Researching prospects at the library, developing direct-mail pieces and other ways to communicate with your target industry, creating brochures, writing journal articles, and attending association meetings will all lead to increased business—but not immediately. Your supervisor must buy in to your goals and methods, or they will never work very well.

It's very important that you create a market profile of the industry that you are targeting. This will help you determine the quality of your target market.

I'm going to take you step by step through a market profile. (This was inspired by Jim Cathcart.) First, take out a clean piece of paper and write "Market Profile" at the top. Then answer the following questions as best you can. This process may take a couple of sittings.

1. The market.
What is the name of the industry or affinity group that you are planning to target?

2. The demographics.
How many potential prospects are there? How many of these companies are there locally, regionally, nationally, and even internationally? Call the associations; they'll tell you. Then find out how many of these companies are big enough for you to do business with, or small enough for you to do business with. For instance, there are about 75,000 printers in the United States, but probably less than a third of them have a sales staff large enough to make it worthwhile for me to prospect them. That's still a big audience to target.

3. Organizations to which they belong.
What national, regional, state, and local associations are involved with this industry? Often there are two or three national associations, and most have local chapters. *The Encyclopedia of Associations* in your library will tell you what you need to know here, and the national associations can give you a list of the smaller chapters.

4. **Publications they read.**

   What publications do they read? Find out by calling the industry associations and by calling the people you already know in the industry.

5. **Meetings they attend.**

   What meetings, conventions, conferences, and trade shows are a part of your target market? Again, you can find this out easily from the associations and from people you already know in the industry.

6. **Who are the industry influencers?**

   Find this out from associations and from people in the industry. Sometimes you can discover the names you need right away, and sometimes it takes some time. Begin with a local scope and then go national when it's appropriate for you. Usually members of the association's board of directors and past presidents are industry influencers. Which are the largest, most successful, most respected businesses? Who is being featured in the industry publications? Every time you meet people in your target industry, ask them who the industry influencers are (besides them, of course).

7. **What are their common needs, fears, and goals?**

   What are the issues of the people within the industry you're trying to target? List these on your market profile. As you learn more, add them to your list. These needs, fears, and goals are the stuff of your positioning strategy. (See Appendix B.) Learn how to speak about the benefits of your product or service in terms of their concerns and goals.

This market profile is critical to giving you a good handle on how best to serve this target industry. Do it now, and revise it every six months or even more often.

There you have it: niche marketing, the fourth cornerstone in building a referral business. This is the most powerful way to create a situation in which you don't have to cold call, you become perceived as an expert in a particular industry as it relates to your product or service, and you develop a reputation. You leverage that expertise and reputation so that people call you, and when you call prospects, they know who you are and want to talk to you.

Work these strategies that I have given you, and your sales will increase *significantly* over the next couple of years. And you'll enjoy the selling process so much more!

Your Referral Castle

The Final Building Blocks

CHAPTER 25

Putting It All Together

By putting the foundation and the four cornerstones of referral selling carefully in place, you will create your referral castle.

Early in this book I quoted noted salesperson Robert Kerrigan, who said, "The way of the world is meeting people through other people." I hope I've demonstrated to you the enormous selling power you can create for yourself when you create great relationships with prospects and customers; serve people well (be they customers, prospects, or referral alliances); and constantly think in terms of how you can leverage those relationships to create more win/win situations that go beyond the buyer/seller relationship.

To create unlimited referrals, you need to engage in expanded thinking. Every business relationship you create has the potential to lead you to other relationships. Thomas Stanley calls this "offering more than the core." Find ways to move your relationships with customers to a level of mutual assistance that goes beyond the core product or service you offer.

When you sell something and gain a new customer, build that relationship so that you can serve each other in ways other than what brought you together in the first place.

That's the leveraging power of relationships. That's *ethical opportunism*—looking for the multiple opportunities in every relationship.

People Will Enjoy Seeing You Succeed

When you serve others well, they will help you. Many people love to have a stake in the success of other people—people like you whom they like and trust.

Not long ago I was teaching my referral strategies to a group of salespeople. The sessions went well, and most of the salespeople started getting more referrals immediately. And those referrals translated into an increase in sales. However, one salesperson, Bruce, was struggling with this referral stuff. He called me and asked if we could meet for breakfast before the next sales meeting.

When we got together, Bruce told me that he wanted to use referrals more but some block was stopping him. With a little exploration, this is what I helped him figure out.

Bruce wanted to be successful by his own efforts—he wanted to "do it himself." Just between you and me, I think he was trying to prove to his father (who was successful and had a very strong personality) that he could do it on his own. For some reason, Bruce felt that asking for referrals—asking for help—was not doing it on his own. So, he found it difficult to ask for referrals.

I helped Bruce reframe his thinking. I asked him, "Do you serve your customers well, so they keep coming back?"

"Yes."

"Do your customers like you and trust you?"

"Yes."

"The times you've gotten referrals without asking, did you convert them into sales and create more happy customers who like you and trust you?"

"Yes."

Then I said, "Who do you think is doing that? You're doing that! You are serving your customers so well, you are creating such good relationships with them, that if you only asked, they would be thrilled to help you. *You* created that. You deserve to be rewarded even more than you are now. These people want to give to you; you just have to get it started."

I'm happy to say that Bruce "got it." He stepped out of his comfort zone a few times to ask for referrals. To his amazement, they came easily. He converted most of those referrals into new customers. For Bruce, the chain reaction has begun. He is now on his way to creating an unlimited supply of referrals, because he now realizes that referrals from his customers are the highest form of praise he can receive. Now it's his goal to create relationships and serve customers so well that they *want* to give him referrals—as soon as he asks!

Working from Referrals Is a Mindset

I can't emphasize this enough. To create unlimited referrals—to build your castle of gold—it has to become your constant way of thinking.

You must constantly say to yourself, "I sell a quality product/service. I deliver incredible service. People like me and trust me. I deserve to get referrals. I serve people so well that they *want* to refer people to me. I deserve this highest form of praise."

The Attitude of Service

Do you have a true attitude of service? Are you constantly looking for ways to serve others?

Are you serving your prospects long before you sell them anything? When you sell someone, do you ask questions that get him thinking in new ways? Do you help him see his situation from new perspectives?

Are you giving referrals to other salespeople? Are you getting to know your customers in such a way that you can bring value to their lives in ways that go far beyond what you sell?

If you are doing these things, then you have the attitude of service and you will have very little difficulty creating unlimited referrals—as long as you remember to ask for them.

If you don't have an attitude of service, your ability to gain referrals will be severely limited.

Zig Ziglar says it this way: "You can get everything in life you want, if you just help enough other people get what they want." And Albert Schweitzer said, "I don't know what your destiny will be, but one thing I know, the only ones among you who will be really happy are those who have sought and found how to serve."

The Power of Leverage

"Master the power of leverage . . . to build real business with long-term strength." So says Bill Brooks, author, speaker, and sales expert. Just as you must have an attitude of service to create unlimited referrals, it helps to have an attitude of leverage.

In his audiotape *Changing the Game: The New Way to Sell* (Nightingale-Conant, 1988), Larry Wilson says this about leverage. "In the past, prospecting was thought of as a funnel. You put a lot of prospects in at the top, and for that effort you end up with a few highly qualified prospects at the bottom. In this scenario, the salesperson's job is to keep the top of the funnel full—activity-intensive prospecting. A lot of time, energy, and money is spent, and of course, most of the suspects who come in at the top never reach the buyer stage.

"Based on the old 'see more people' belief, it confuses activity with accomplishment.

"In this new model . . . the question changes from, 'How can I make this sale?' to 'How can I make this sale *and* how can this relationship lead me to other business?' This point of view is to never prospect for just one shot, one sale business."

I couldn't have said it better myself. Thanks, Larry! If you aspire to build a base of satisfied customers and referral alliances, you can constantly tap into this base for more business. This is leverage! Now, instead of "activity-intensive prospecting," you have "strategic planning prospecting."

Wilson goes on to say, "Be careful of spending time with business that has no leveragability. No business should pass through you without putting it to the leveragability test." From my perspective, this doesn't mean you don't take nonleveragable business. It means that you are always looking for this leverage angle, right from the beginning of each relationship. If you have this new awareness, or attitude of leverage, you're more likely to see the opportunities.

> **"Master the power**
>
> **of leverage . . .**
>
> **to build real**
>
> **business with**
>
> **long-term strength."**
>
> *Bill Brooks*

Please understand that the leverage I'm talking about is not manipulation or going for lopsided wins. Leveraging relationships should always be a two-way, win/win proposition. Getting your customers to provide referrals to you—to "sell" for you—is the greatest leverage in the world of selling.

A Solid Foundation and Cornerstones

I'd like to remind you of the essence of each section of this book. With that, I'll leave the rest up to you.

First, we laid the foundation by talking about two fundamentals in selling: relationships and service. The *relationship* allows everything else to occur. The *attitude of service* helps you build a trusting relationship in which each party can keep winning for years to come.

Then we covered the four cornerstones of building your referral business. The first cornerstone is "exceed your customers' expectations." There are three main thoughts I want to leave you with on this topic.

1. To exceed your customers' expectations, you have to know what their expectations are. You have to discover why you got their business, how the other guy lost their business, what it will take to keep them

happy, and what it will take to make them unhappy.
With this knowledge, you can make them say
"Wow" when you serve them.

2. Be ready, willing, and able to "be in the problems."
   When a problem arises, don't even flinch. Just be
   there and start working through the solution as best
   you can. Make it easy for them to complain; in fact,
   encourage it. Remember, a relationship that's had a
   problem that's been handled well is a stronger relationship than one that's never had a problem. You
   can brag about your problem-free relationships, but
   if I were you, I'd brag about the relationships in
   which you fixed the problems.

3. Help them reduce their stress. Make dealing with
   you an oasis in their busy lives. Anticipate their
   needs, discover their stresses, and serve them beyond
   their expectations.

The second cornerstone is "form referral alliances." Identify
the people (and other businesses) in your world who have
the ability to refer business to you, even though they may
never become customers themselves, and find ways to meet
more of these types of people. Make sure they know what
you do and how you truly benefit others. Make sure *you*
know what they do and how they truly benefit others. Then
find ways to continually serve each other. Network with the
best networkers. Network with centers of influence and
you'll become a center of influence!

Steven Sullivan sums it up well. "As I reflected back on
all the great salesmen I've known, a common thread ran
through the fabric of their individual selling style. No, it is
not creativity, intelligence, sense of urgency, or communication skills. What they share with each other is an ability to
build a successful network, a group of individuals whom
they motivate to support and sustain their efforts. They recognize they are not an island unto themselves. They realize
no matter how great their individual talent, it pales in com-

parison to a supporting cast." Richard Weylman says, "Successful people are interdependent, not independent."

The third cornerstone is "prospect for referrals." Take control of your destiny (as much as any mortal can) and be proactive in gaining referrals. When you ask for referrals, do so in a way that lets your sources know it's important to you. Ask for their help. Upgrade the referral as much as possible. To help your sources protect their relationship with their friend or colleague, see if they want to call the prospect before you do. Always keep your referral sources informed of the progress of the referral, and always keep them well thanked.

Finally, the fourth cornerstone is "target niche markets." When you create a reputation in a target industry, the referrals will flow effortlessly. Having expertise in a target industry will allow you to bring value to the table that none of your competitors can. Pick an industry you like and create a reputation for yourself. You'll have more fun, and the referrals and sales will truly be unlimited.

Network with the best networkers. Network with centers of influence and *you'll* become a center of influence!

Work on any one of these cornerstones and referrals will come your way. Work a little on all four and you'll build a strong house of referrals. Master all four cornerstones and you'll build a castle of referrals—unlimited referrals.

Dear Reader,

I'm done and you're just getting started. I've given you my best in this book. Now it's your turn to give it your best. It's time for you to take action on some of the ideas I've presented here.

Let me suggest that you find one, two, or three strategies you can implement right away—and then do it! The sooner you begin to act on specific things, the more likely you will act at all.

Just because you've already read this book doesn't mean you can't go back and read some of it again to remind yourself of other strategies you liked. In fact, why don't you put a reminder in your calendar for, say, six months from now, to pick up the book again. You'll be amazed at what new things you'll be ready to make part of your selling repertoire.

I've given you my knowledge. But I can't make you act, and I can't give you the burning desire to make your actions powerful. That will have to come from you!

If you ever have any questions regarding what I've written here, don't hesitate to give me a call or write me a letter. We'll chat about it. Also, if you have any success stories using referrals, share them with me. Maybe I'll put them in a revised edition of the book and make you famous for all time.

I wish you great success,

Bill

Bill

2915 FENIMORE ROAD, SILVER SPRING, MD 20902-2600

Appendices

More Ideas for Gaining Referrals

In addition to all the ideas presented thus far, there are other ways you and your company can increase the referrals you receive. I have personally seen businesses using every one of them to great success. See which ones you can use right away. Then come back to this section in six months and see which others you can adopt and adapt. Some approaches may not be ideal for your particular business. In that case, use some creative thinking to adapt them to your world.

Give Thank-You Gifts That Get Them Talking About You

Whenever I do a significant piece of business for a client, I send a thank-you gift. I have a few generic items, but I prefer personalized gifts. I call my clients' assistant, or the receptionist, or whomever I can find, and ask them about my client's hobbies and special interests. Then I pick up an affordable gift to send. Then when I follow up to see if they were satisfied with my programs, they are usually very receptive to my request for referrals—or probing for more business opportunities with them.

The more personalized the gift is, the less money you need to spend. People are more impressed when you spend some time and thoughtful, creative energy on it. Here are some examples:

I recently sent a captain's shirt to a gentleman who loves boating.

I sent three cookbooks that my old company published to a sales manager because he likes to cook.

My client and now friend Phil Boland is a principal in a commercial printing company and he has a penchant for gorillas. In fact, he prints T-shirts for all of his employees that have a gorilla face on the front and the words "PRESS ON" on the back. I know it sounds a little strange, but his people enjoy his unique brand of enthusiasm. So I went to a toy store and bought a little toy gorilla. I had a trophy shop prepare a base with an engraved plate that read "PRESS ON." He loved it! He appreciated my creativity—and it led to more business and a growing friendship.

A sales manager named Steve has developed a special interest in all things Disney because Disney is one of his larger accounts. After two successful workshops I did for his company, I sent Steve an audiotape album of the complete musical works of Disney. Two days later he called me and said, "Bill, I don't know if your timing is always this perfect, but I received your tapes this morning and my Disney contact is coming in for a meeting this afternoon. I've already got a tape in the boom box. As we enter the conference room, the tape will be playing 'Whistle While You Work.' Thanks!"

IMPORTANT! If you follow up with your customers to make sure they received your gift, don't ask for referrals at that time. The gift will appear less sincere. I know this because I blew it once with a customer. I suspect he thought my request was tied to the gift, and he was a fairly contained individual. I should have waited for a few more opportunities to serve him, to gain his trust, before I asked.

What can you give satisfied customers to thank them for their business and to get them talking about you to others?

Create a Special Gift Certificate

Here's an idea that will get your satisfied customers saying good things about you behind your back. I have coached several businesses to use a special kind of gift certificate to increase referrals. Here's how it works.

Create a gift certificate for your products or services that you give to your satisfied customers, who must then pass it on to a new potential customer. This creates what I call a triple win. It's a win for the new customer, because he gets to do business with you at a first-time discount. It's a win for your existing customer, because she gets to help out a friend or colleague. And, of course, it's a win for you because you have a satisfied customer talking about you and encouraging people to try you. This will have a direct impact on your sales!

Host an Educational Event

Invite customers and referral alliances to an educational program, and ask them to bring a guest or two—free. This event must have real value. It must be a real opportunity for people to learn valuable information and, perhaps, network with others. You may already be hosting this type of learning event, but have you asked your customers or referral alliances to bring guests? Treat everyone like royalty, and these guests will see what it's like doing business with you and your company.

Stay in Touch and Keep Planting Seeds

Staying in touch with your customers is the bridge between serving them well and having them give you referrals. I've already described Marilyn Jennings's use of champagne baskets. In her book, she tells of a car salesperson who sends pumpkins to all his customers just before Halloween. With those pumpkins, he plants the seed (pardon the pun) that he values their referrals. She also tells of an insurance salesperson who has baskets of Easter eggs delivered to his clients at Easter time.

Do you send birthday cards to your customers? Holiday cards? How about sending cards when others don't? I know several companies that send cards on Valentine's Day: "We love our customers." Maybe you can send an anniversary card each year on the date you and your customer started doing business together.

Jimmy Jacobs, CLU, ChFC, a very successful insurance agent, sends birthday cards to his clients' children with coupons from a local ice-cream parlor. He gets the coupons for free, because usually Mom and Dad buy cones as well. For out-of-town clients, he puts a stick of gum in the birthday card.

What creative things can you do to stay in touch and continue to plant seeds for referrals, as well as for future business from your business relationships?

Give Out Samples

Have your customers, referral alliances, and even your friends give out a free sample related to your product or service. If you learn that a customer or referral alliance will be attending an event with lots of other prospects present—such as a chamber of commerce or an association meeting—equip him with some samples to distribute. Then you can be proactive and follow up with a phone call to your customer asking him to remember a few people at the meeting who received a sample. I once had a customer ask me for my promotional literature to pass out at a meeting of his colleagues. I made two sales as a direct result. You can't buy that kind of advertising.

Not every satisfied customer will be willing to do this, but many will. You just have to create a relationship that makes them want to toot your horn.

What can you give to your outgoing satisfied customers that they can, in turn, give to others?

Adopt Orphans

The sales term "orphan" is most widely used in the insurance industry. An orphan is a policy holder whose agent is no longer with the company. These orphan accounts have great potential for more business, if they are adopted and cared for.

Does your business have these types of orphan accounts? If so, adopt as many as you can. Many of them are easy sources for more business as well as great referrals—if you serve them well and ask for referrals!

Use a Newsletter

You probably already know that a regular newsletter can be a great way to stay in touch with customers and prospects. Make sure at least 80 percent of your newsletter's content is information your contact can use. Keep the chatter about you and your company to a minimum.

At the same time, in every issue, plant seeds for referrals. One effective method is a little box with a headline that reads, "Do you know of anyone else who might enjoy receiving this newsletter?" Readers can fill out the coupon and mail it back to you or give you a call to get a subscription. This is a referral. Call the current newsletter recipient and learn a little about this new prospect before calling him or her. (Upgrade the referral.)

Every now and then, call some of your customers or prospects. Ask them, "Are you receiving the newsletter? Do you get the time to read it? Are you enjoying it? Whom do you know who would enjoy a complimentary subscription? Great, why them?"

Speak and Grow Rich

Many studies have shown that people's #1 fear is public speaking. Yet it's a very important component in establishing a reputation that will bring you lots of referrals. In fact, becoming skilled at delivering a program to a group of people is by far the most powerful way to create a reputation within a target industry. If you're not afraid of speaking in front of groups, do it. If you are afraid, then join Toastmasters, go to Dale Carnegie, or take a night class in public speaking. Overcome your fear, because speaking to a room full of prospects creates a room full of warm referrals.

Local, state, regional, and national associations have meetings. They bring people together and they use speakers. Often the speakers don't get paid, but if you're in a room full of 100 or 200 prospects, you don't need to get paid. All you need to do is demonstrate your knowledge, ability, confidence, and trustworthiness. Educate your audience with your knowledge and experience; entertain them just enough to keep their keen attention; and entice them to want to know more.

No matter what your subject, tell some stories and give real-life examples. It's amazing to watch the audience energy and attention increase as you shift into an anecdote or example. The fun that you bring to a program helps people absorb your information.

Most of the time, you can get the list of attendees. If you're any good at speaking, then calling this list is like calling very warm referrals. They know you're good, they know what you do, and they are more than willing to have a conversation with you. Your voice-mail messages to them will get returned.

If you can't get a list of attendees (or even if you can), try to get a business card from everybody in the room. I usually come up with a little prize for a quick business raffle. I buy a book or something that relates to their industry, or maybe just something fun, like a huge candy bar. If you have a product or a service that you can actually give away, better yet. Because it's a prize, you now have an easy and professional way to mention your product or service within the context of your talk.

Have everyone drop a business card in a basket. Get an assistant to pass the basket around. Then give away a prize or two. This helps you determine the prospects in the room and adds liveliness to the talk. You might ask your audience to write on the back of their cards things that frustrate them about their industry or about their business, especially as it relates to your topic. You can use what they write in your speech if you're a skilled speaker.

After the program, wade through the cards, sorting out the few good prospects from the rest. You now have their names and phone numbers and their challenges. They know who you are. They know you are an expert. Your call becomes a warm call. Public speaking is one of the best things you can do for your referral selling.

To improve your speaking skills, contact Toastmasters International at 800-937-7325 or Dale Carnegie at 800-232-5800. Tell them you're interested in their public speaking program. If you are already speaking regularly as part of your profession, join the National Speakers Association at 602-968-2552.

Get Someone to Blow Your Horn

I'll bet you have one or more customers who believe in the value you bring to people and who might really enjoy telling others. Ask them to write a letter about you and send it to everyone they know. This may sound like pie in the sky, but it's happened to me. I used to conduct an assembly program for elementary school children. I would tell stories, sing a little, do a magic trick, and in that fun atmosphere, teach them a little about goal setting and try to contribute to their self-esteem.

A woman from the gifted and talented program of a particular school district attended one of my assemblies. She was so effusive in her praise that I took a risk. I asked if she thought the other schools should know about my program. Of course, she said yes. Then I asked if there was any kind of interdistrict memo system that I could tap into. The result: she wrote a memo to every elementary school principal in her county. That memo brought me many opportunities to visit schools in that district for several years.

Over the past few years, I have been doing work for a printing company in Baltimore whose president is an industry influencer. He is so pleased with my work with his sales force that without my asking, he offered to write a letter for me to the rest of the industry, taking advantage of his increasing visibility and influence. He wrote a great letter. I've already used it to bring in new business. And he has talked about me to so many people that he has been a significant factor in my increased success within his industry. (Thanks, Jerry!)

You've probably received a letter or two from people you know touting the worthiness of someone with whom they've done business. This could range from a half-dozen letters to a grand mailing to any substantial lists your clients may have.

Do you have any satisfied customers who might do something like this for you? Take the risk and ask.

Be Creative in Rewarding Customers for Referrals

We've already seen what Joe Girard does with his bird-dog system. I know a massage therapist named Hershel who gives away a free visit to every customer who brings in a new customer. Hershel charges $60 a massage. An average customer comes for at least 12 visits (some return many more times). So Hershel gives away a $60 visit (not his true cost) for $720 worth of business.

What can you do to reward your customers who give you referrals? Here are just a few ideas: books, flowers, contributions to charity in their name, restaurant gift certificates. Get creative and come up with rewards tailored to your industry.

These are just a sampling of the many creative ideas you can use to stay in touch with your customers, plant seeds for referrals, and generate great word-of-mouth. Read these over again. Maybe you can't use an idea just as I've presented it. But with some creative thinking, you and your co-workers can adapt one or more to your world. The result: more referrals—the most powerful way to sell.

How Are You Positioned in the Marketplace?

I n 1981, a book was published that revolutionized the way companies promote their products and services. *Positioning: The Battle for Your Mind* (McGraw-Hill, 1981) by Jack Trout and Al Ries changed the face of Madison Avenue advertising strategies forever. This change has trickled down to how you and I must think about how we position our product or service in the minds of our prospects, customers, and referral alliances.

Trout and Ries proved that it's no longer enough to tout the features and benefits of a product. In our overcommunicated society, our minds are constantly under attack from advertising. You see it everywhere: on taxicabs and buses, on TV and radio, in movies, billboards, your mail, even on T-shirts and other clothing. Everywhere you look, someone is promoting something. Because of this, the authors contend, our minds are "full." We can't hold any more. If a company wants a foothold in our mind, it will have to push someone else out first.

Well, I'm not sure I agree that our minds are full, but I do agree that it is very difficult to catch people's attention and deliver a message that will truly stick in their minds.

Trout and Ries say that people rank products and services on mental ladders, and that whoever occupies the top rung holds the high ground. The product, service, company, or person who owns the lead position in the prospect's mind is the one that is remembered and patronized.

Be the First if You Can

The first rule of positioning is to get into the mind first to be the first one who does what you do, sells what you sell. The first in the mind is almost impossible to unseat. Who was the first man to run the mile in under four minutes? Roger Bannister—most people have heard of him. But who was the second? Who was the first woman to fly solo across the Atlantic Ocean? Amelia Earhart. But who was the second?

You can see the power of being first. As Trout and Ries say, "It's good to have the best product, but it's even better to be the first into the mind." Whenever you are first in your industry or geographic area with a new product, service, technology, or process, make sure you get into people's minds quickly and in a big way. Establish your leadership position, deliver more than you promised, and you will be the standard by which others are measured.

But what if you aren't the first? What if you are selling in an established and very competitive arena, where being the first is not really an option?

Don't Go Head to Head

The second rule of positioning is not to go head to head with your competition. Find a way to position your product/service that makes it different from what is already in customers' minds. This is accomplished with a positioning strategy that is reflected by a positioning statement. The simpler the strategy and statement, the better.

If you want people to remember you, remember that you are trying to stick your message into very cluttered brains. The more simple and clear the positioning statement, the better chance it has of taking hold.

Shift Your Focus

The principles of positioning shift your promotional focus from the product/service to the prospects' minds. The product/service must be promoted in relationship to what's already in the mind. Unless your product/service is so different that it creates a completely new ladder, you must first be aware of the ladder that's already there.

For instance, the sales of 7UP were modest when it was being promoted as a "lemon-lime soft drink." Sales skyrocketed when it was positioned against the leaders (Coke and Pepsi) as the "Uncola."

Avis, the car rental company, positioned itself against the leader, Hertz, not by going head to head, but by acknowledging its second-place standing and turning that into an advantage: "We try harder!"

As you can see, sometimes a positioning statement will state what you are not before it says what you are. This is one way you can begin to position yourself against what is already in the mind of your prospect.

How Do You Benefit People?

How does all this relate to you and referral selling? Referral selling means generating word-of-mouth. It means that your prospects, customers, and referral alliances must know exactly what it is you do and how it benefits people.

When you meet with a referral alliance, ask, "Do you know anybody else who does what I do?" See what's already in her mind with regard to your product/service. See what position it holds. See how you compare. Then make sure your referral alliance knows how you are different, and how that difference benefits people. Don't try to go head to head with what's already in her mind. Don't say "we are the best," or "we deliver the highest quality." These superlatives don't have much power, because everyone uses them. Rather, say, "what makes us different is . . ." or "we are the only company that. . . ." If you claim superiority, explain how and why with both the facts and great enthusiasm, so your alliances will have that enthusiasm as they refer you to others.

For instance, maybe there is a real advantage to people that your company is smaller than the leaders. If that's so, exploit your smallness. A perfect example came from Glenn, who attended one of my seminars. Before I met him, Glenn worked for a small advertising agency with sales of $4 million. He was trying to get an appointment with a prospect, but to no avail. Then he found a creative way to position his company against the giants.

Glen bought two fish bowls and two fish. He put the small fish in the large bowl and attached a sign to the bowl that read "$20 Million Agency." He put the large fish in the small bowl and added a sign that read "$4 Million Agency." He delivered the bowls to this hard-to-reach prospect with a note that read, "Which fish would you rather be?" He got the appointment. This is positioning at its best: a simple concept, delivered very creatively.

Your positioning doesn't always have to be delivered in such a creative way. In fact, the simpler, the better. In the words of Trout and Ries, your positioning strategy must be "a simple concept, with simple words, expressed in a straightforward manner." That's what will stick in people's minds.

Focus on the Other Person

When you create your strategy and corresponding statement, remember that it does not start with you, your product/service, or your company. It begins in the mind of your prospect, customer, or referral alliance. What is already in there? The people who created the Uncola campaign did not start with 7UP. They began by considering what products already occupied the top rung of the mental ladder (Coke and Pepsi).

Positioning is best done by two or more people. In *Think and Grow Rich,* Napoleon Hill explained that when two minds come together, a mastermind is created that comes up with ideas and perspectives that the two minds could not create separately. You are probably too close to your product/ service to come up with the best positioning strategy on your own. Bring in people with a more neutral perspective to help you formulate your strategy and statement.

Remember, trying to be all things to all people is the kiss of death in today's marketplace. To position yourself effectively, you must be willing to sacrifice potential markets in exchange for capturing real customers. With a narrow focus, you give up the universe, but you gain a strong hold on people's minds. The net result will be an easier marketing plan and increased sales.

Here are a few positioning strategies that I ran across in my local business journals:

- GEICO (car insurance) insures only drivers with good driving records. The benefit to prospects and customers is lower rates.

- A commercial real estate agent in Purcellville, Virginia, specializes in finding lower-rent storefront properties for new businesses. Business is booming. The benefit to the customer is easier entry into retail business. The benefit to the town is a resurgence in the downtown shopping district.

- A fish farmer in Virginia has positioned himself as Frank Perdue, but marketing fresh fish instead of chicken. This strategy conveys the scope of business he is trying to build.

In a short article in the *Washington Business Journal*, Alf Nucifora shared five rules for selecting a position using a unique point of difference.

1. Analyze the marketplace and your competitors carefully. What's different about their company or product? How can you be different from them?

2. Analyze your own business product or service. What do you have to say about yourself that is unique? And what do you have that the marketplace needs?

3. Pick a positioning that is simple, easy to assimilate, and, if possible, unique.

4. Try to keep your positioning consistent in style (in look, format, typeface, logo treatment, and so on).

5. Remember, it's important to establish your positioning from day one. If you don't have one, develop one now and stay with it over time. Be consistent in content.

Now it's your turn. Begin to strategize your position in the marketplace and in the minds of your prospects, customers, and referral alliances. Get some help to come up with a simple concept, expressed in a straightforward manner, so that what you do and what you sell will stick in the mind of everyone you encounter. When you accomplish this, every seed you plant can take root and will eventually bear fruit for you.

Bibliography
& Index

Bibliography

More Building Blocks in These Books and Tapes

The following books and audiotapes are quoted in this book. Every one of them contains great material. Most can be ordered from any bookstore. In many cases, I provide a phone number for direct ordering.

Alessandra, Tony. *Non-Manipulative Selling.* (Fireside, 1987). Order from Alessandra & Associates, 800-222-4383.

Burg, Bob. *Endless Referrals: Network Your Everyday Contacts into Sales.* (McGraw-Hill, 1994). Order from Burg Communications, 800-726-3667.

Cathcart, Jim. *Relationship Selling.* (Perigee Books, 1990). Order from Jim Cathcart Company, 800-222-4883.

Cooper, Donald. *Human Marketing: How to Become the Preferred Supplier of What You Sell.* (audiotape program) (The Donald Cooper Corp., 1995). Order from The Donald Cooper Corp., 416-260-8295.

Gandolfo, Joe, and Donal Jay Korn. *Sell and Grow Rich* (Dearborn Financial Publishing, 1993). Order from Dearborn, 800-437-9002.

Girard, Joe. *How to Sell Anything to Anybody.* (Warner Books, 1977).Order from Joe Girard, 810-774-9020.

Gitomer, Jeffrey. *The Sales Bible.* (Morrow, 1994). Order from Business Marketing Services, 800-242-5388.

Glanz, Barbara. *Building Customer Loyalty.* (Irwin Professional Publishing, 1994). Order from Irwin, 800-634-3963.

Hill, Napoleon. *Think and Grow Rich.* (Fawcett Crest, revised edition, 1960).

Hopkins, Tom. *How to Master the Art of Selling.* (Tom Hopkins International, 1982).

Hyken, Shep. *Moments of Magic: Be a Star with Your Customers and Keep Them Forever.* (The Alan Press, 1993). Order from Shepard Presentations, 314-692-2200.

Jennings, Marilyn. *Championship Selling.* (MCJ Publishing, 1986). Order from Richard Flint, 804-873-7722.

Kramnick, Scott. *Expecting Referrals.* (Associates Publishing, 1993). Order from Sharing Success Seminars, 800-786-9799.

Liswood, Laura. *Serving Them Right: Innovative and Powerful Customer Retention Strategies.* (Harper Business, 1990).

Levitt, Theodore. *The Marketing Imagination.* (Free Press, 1986).

Mackay, Harvey. *Beware the Naked Man Who Offers You His Shirt.* (Morrow, 1990).

Mackay, Harvey. *How to Build a Network of Power Relationships.* (audiotape) (Nightingale-Conant, 1995). Order from Nightingale-Conant, 800-525-9000.

Mackay, Harvey. *The Rolodex Network Builder.* (Mackay Envelope Corp., 1993). Order from Mackay Envelope Corp., 612-331-9311.

Mackay, Harvey. *Swim With the Sharks Without Being Eaten Alive.* (Morrow, 1988)

Misner, Ivan. *The World's Best-Known Marketing Secret: Building Your Business with Word-of-Mouth Marketing.* (Bard & Stephen, 1994). Order from Paradigm Productions, 800-688-9394.

Munro, Barry Graham. *Smart Salespeople Sometimes Wear Plaid.* (Prima, 1994).

Rinke, Wolf. *Make It a Winning Life.* (Achievement Publishers, 1992). Order from Wolf Rinke Associates, 800-828-WOLF.

Sewell, Carl, and Paul Brown. *Customers for Life: How to Turn That One-Time Buyer into a Lifetime Customer.* (Doubleday, 1990).

Sheer, Mark. *Referrals.* (Mark Sheer Seminars, 1993). Order from Sheer Seminars, 714-588-5931.

Stanley, Thomas. *Networking with the Affluent.* (Irwin Professional Publishing, 1996). Order from Irwin, 800-634-3963.

Sullivan, Steven D. *Selling at Mach 1.* (Motivational Resources, 1994). Order from Motivational Resources, 203-438-5952.

Trout, Jack, and Al Ries. *Positioning: The Battle for Your Mind.* (McGraw-Hill, 1981).

Waymon, Lynne, and Anne Baber. *Great Connections: Small Talk and Networking for Business People.* (Impact Publications, 1992). Order from Lynne Waymon, 800-352-2939.

Waymon, Lynne, and Anne Baber. *52 Ways to Reconnect, Follow Up, and Stay in Touch, When You Don't Have Time to Network.* (Kendall/Hunt Publishing, 1994). Order from Lynne Waymon, 800-352-2939.

Weylman, C. Richard. *Opening Closed Doors: Keys to Reaching Hard-to-Reach People.* (Irwin Professional Publishing, 1994). Order from The Achievement Group, 800-535-4332.

Wilson, Larry. *Changing the Game: The New Way to Sell.* (audiotape) (Nightingale-Conant, 1988). Order from Nightingale-Conant, 800-525-9000.

Winninger, Tom. *Price Wars.* (St. Thomas Press, 1994). Order from St. Thomas Press, 800-899-8971.

Index

Here's What Others Are Saying About Bill's Seminars and Speeches . . .

"It's been about 15 months since the program you delivered to our advisors and your program has had a lasting impact. Our advisors are acquiring new clients by referrals at a rate that's 40% higher than the national average for our company. Thanks for laying such a strong foundation to build on."

Tim Holland, District Manager
American Express Financial Advisors

"Bill's referral system and his presentation style are both top grade. Our agents gave him a standing ovation, which was well deserved."

Peter Hearst, General Agent
Northwestern Mutual Life

"A month has passed since your seminar at our agency and people are still excited. You actually changed people's thinking regarding referrals . . . and that has changed their actions. We definitely will use you again."

Steve Suddeth, General Agent
MassMutual

"My entire staff of account officers is now charged with your 'Referral Mindset.' I tried a new idea I learned from you the evening following your program and I was amazed how well it worked with my client. Thanks for firing-up my people about referrals."

William Driscoll, Sr. Vice President
NationsBank

"WOW!!! Your presentation here at Burton & Mayer last weekend was absolutely outstanding. Pete Arvan, our top producer, told me this, 'When I got up this morning, I couldn't figure out what Bill was going to do for six hours, but when the time ran out, I still wanted more!'"

Timothy J. Burton, President
Burton & Mayer, Inc.